Early Praise for *Elevate the Core*

I have found teacher training in Christian Education to be invaluable. It not only helped me conduct more organized and engaging adult Sunday school classes, but it also helped me learn how to formulate lessons plans and course curriculum in Christian education. I even used the skills I gained through the teacher training in CORE to write lesson commentaries for different published adult Sunday school books and Bible commentaries as well as exposition papers I had to write for the biblical studies course I took later in seminary. I have taught an introductory speech course for City Colleges of Chicago for over thirteen years, and the teacher training received in Christian education even improved my teaching in the college classroom.

J. Garrison
Adjunct Professor
Harold Washington College

I had the pleasure of being part of the first group to experience the Elevate the Core training. I am a lay person who is a professional in the healthcare industry but have a gift from God and a love for teaching young people. The process was not easy. It required searching the Word of God and uncovered things about our spiritual maturity. With the educational process and deep soul searching, this process was transformational! There was growth that would not have occurred otherwise.

Melissa L. Zinnerman RN, MSN
Apostolic Faith Church

Dr. Rosa Sailes believes, and has demonstrated in many ways, that teaching is a special gift that requires training, study, and prayer. This allowed us to expand our Christian education department to the standard it is today, blessing the lives of many people through the enrichment of teachers with this special training.

Evangelist Ada B. Landry, M.A.
Elective Superintendent
Apostolic Church of God

Rosa Sailes has vast experience both as a secular and Christian educator. She has a heart to give teachers in-depth training to strengthen their Christian ministry. I, along with other leaders and teachers, trained in the in-depth classes to prepare ourselves and other teachers to increase our biblical knowledge and skills in order to better equip our congregants—and it works.

Elder Maurice Landry, M.A.
Elective Lead Bible Study Teacher
Apostolic Church of God

Ongoing Christian education training opened my eyes to concepts and thought processes that I really needed but thought I already received in seminary. The training I received under Dr. Sailes' leadership exposed me to exceptional teaching that benefited my ministry in unimaginable ways.

Tim Lee
Director, Housing & Residence Life
Chicago State University

ROSA SAILES, ED.D., M.T.S.

A Call to Transform the
Christian Education Ministry

ELEVATE THE
CORE

KEYS in the
KINGDOM
PUBLISHING

Printed in the United States of America

Publisher: Keys to the Kingdom Publishing, LLC
P.O. Box 2812
Bristol, CT 06011
1-800-912-6282
www.ktkpublishing.com

Cover Design by Trinidad Zavala

Library of Congress Control Number: 2018949290

ISBN 9780985465421

I offer this book to God, who gives me strength and whose grace has blessed me exceedingly above all I could ask or think.

⁓

I dedicate this volume with love and thanks to my mother, Bessie Jordan, who taught me to know God; my aunt Julia Clark, who showed me the power of writing and reading; my brother, Antoine Jordan, whose teaching pushes me to study harder; the late Bishop Arthur M. Brazier, who supported the vision of education with passion and power; and the teachers and staff of the Apostolic Church of God Sunday Morning Bible Study, whose energy and hard work brought the CORE to life.

Contents

Foreword 7

Preface: A Cause for Concern 10

ONE—Elevate: The Need to Change Perspectives

Chapter 1: The Case for Teaching in the Church 14

Chapter 2: The State of the Teaching Ministry...23

Chapter 3: The Divine Nature of Congregational Teaching..................36

TWO—Foundations: The Catalysts of Transformation

Chapter 4: The Five Features: Essentials of Christian Learning 45

Chapter 5: Pillar 1 - Teacher Knowledge 56

Chapter 6: Pillar 2 - Bible-Centered Teaching...74

Chapter 7: Pillar 3 - Spirit-Led Encounters 88

Chapter 8: Pillar 4 - Authentic Engagement 107

THREE—CORE: An Approach to Sustainable Teacher Preparation

Chapter 9: C – Call: Recognizing the Call 120

Chapter 10: O – Orientation: Exploring the Teacher Process............127

Chapter 11: R – Refining: Furthering Knowledge and Skill................152

Chapter 12: E – Enrichment: Strengthening the Ministry 164

Conclusion: Realizing the Power of an Elevated CORE 173

Appendix A: Survey Questions...181

Appendix B: The RISE Model...185

Endnotes 188

Foreword

IN MATTHEW 28:18-20, Jesus gave His final marching orders to His disciples, orders to be followed not only by the group assembled on the mountain at the time He was taken up into heaven, but also to be carried out by everyone who would become a disciple throughout history—including today. On this occasion, Jesus stated,

> *All authority in heaven and on earth has been given to me. Therefore go and make disciples of all nations, baptizing them in the name of the Father and of the Son and of the Holy Spirit, and teaching them to obey everything I have commanded you. And surely I am with you always to the very end of the age. (Matthew 28:18-20, NIV)*

These commands of Christ have never been rescinded or modified. Therefore, based on the authority, power, and presence of Jesus (through the Holy Spirit), we who follow Him and comprise His church today are to respond by taking the specific actions mentioned. So, what are we to do? What is involved in making disciples? Discipleship is a transformational, Spirit-enabled *process* that begins with an initial commitment to Jesus Christ as Savior and Lord of life in positive response to the Gospel, follows with public identification with Christ through baptism, then continues to move forward in lifelong, day-by-day growth that reinforces the relational commitment.

The greatest facilitator and evidence of the growth process is unconditional obedience to the will of God as revealed in Scripture. Because obedience is so critical to the discipleship process, Jesus specifically mentions not only the fact of obedience, but also the basic tool to use to facilitate obedience in the lives of Christ-followers—teaching. At this point, it must be made clear that the type of teaching Jesus has in mind is not just filling people's minds with information, but guiding them through a life of ongoing transformation.

Facilitating the transformational process, with regard to both initial commitment and ongoing growth, involves four steps:

1. Helping people become *aware* of the truth.
2. Helping people *understand* the truth.
3. Helping people *apply* and personally *take ownership* of the truth.
4. Helping people *communicate* the truth to others.

Movement through this process does not "just happen." There must be an intentional, clearly defined strategy at the local church level to most effectively carry out God's plan. Fortunately, God has not only told us what to do; He has also provided a supernatural, Spirit-empowered ministry model for *implementing* His plan—spiritual gifts. Ephesians 4:11-16 gives a description:

> *It was he who gave some to be apostles, some to be prophets, some to be evangelists, and some to be pastors and teachers, to prepare God's people for works of service, so that the body of Christ may be built up, until we all reach unity in the faith and in the knowledge of the Son of God and become mature, attaining to the whole measure of the fullness of Christ. Then we will no longer be infants, tossed back and forth by the waves, and blown here and there by every wind of teaching and by the cunning and craftiness of men in their deceitful scheming. Instead, speaking the truth in love, we will in all things grow up into him who is the Head, that is, Christ. From him the whole body, joined and held together by every supporting ligament, grows and builds itself up in love, as each part does its work. (NIV)*

The responsibility of local church leadership is to work within God's design of spiritual gifting, to most effectively identify, equip, launch, nurture, encourage, and grow those who have been given the spiritual gift of teaching. While such a task is intensive and demanding, the cost to the body of Christ for failure to seriously deal with the issue is extremely high: lack of spiritual maturity, lack of spiritual reproduction, and openness to spiritual deception and destruction.

Within the pages of this book, Rosa Sailes provides foundational principles upon which a local church can expand and build an effective, long-term teacher preparation and equipping ministry. These principles are not idealistic, untested theory. Rather, they flow out of many years of ministry experience "in the trenches." Such an overview of the educational ministry landscape will give teaching ministry planners an awareness of issues that need to be addressed.

Dr. Sailes has also rightly understood the critical point that effective equipping for teaching ministry must focus *first* on the Bible teacher's own relationship with God and their motivation for teaching, then move to methodology, resources, and skill development. There must be a humble, servant-oriented heart and a constant sense of *total* dependence on God.

So, as you prepare to engage this book, pray. Ask God to *first* touch *your* heart and reveal where *you* need to be in relationship with Him. Then, ask God for wisdom to understand the concepts presented and how those concepts could be implemented in your church setting. Finally, ask God to use *you*, in *any* way He chooses, to facilitate maximum teaching ministry effectiveness in the context in which He has sovereignly placed you.

Dale A. Johnson, PhD
Retired Adjunct Professor of Educational Ministry
Moody Bible Institute, Chicago, Illinois

PREFACE: A CAUSE FOR CONCERN

AN INCREASING NUMBER OF PASTORS are removing Sunday school and other Christian education programs from the menu of options available in their churches. While I am grieved about that, this book is not about saving Sunday school from the pastoral chopping block.[1] I am grieved because this trend suggests a larger issue: the diminishing respect for teaching in local congregations.[2] The data indicates that the negative plight of teaching is evident in church communities and denominations across the United States.

Much of today's teaching in the church—particularly around basic Bible knowledge and our collective identity as Christians—has traditionally been conducted by lay members of the congregation. Their work is considered informal because of the belief that the responsibility for teaching rests with the senior pastor and other professional clergy. There is no doubt that the pastor and the pastoral staff are key in preparing the congregation to live out the faith. *Elevate the CORE* does not make an argument to diminish the role of pastoral leadership or the clergy who are charged with local guidance. Yet, the idea that *only* professional clergy should be responsible for congregational teaching limits the ability of any assembly to fully engage the gifts the Holy Spirit has given to the church. *Elevate the CORE* makes the case for revitalizing Christian education programs through a more inclusive teaching ministry.

Elevate the CORE is divided into three sections. The first section examines current perceptions of congregational teaching. **Chapter one** makes the case for the teaching ministry as a critical work of the church. **Chapter two** provides an overview of congregational teaching today. **Chapter three** examines the teaching ministry as a spiritual gift and call. Section two discusses the anchors of Christian education. **Chapter four** names the five features of Christian learning. **Chapters five through eight** explain each of the four pillars of Christian teaching that connect Christian education and spiritual transformation. **Chapters nine through twelve** in section three outline the CORE approach to sustainable teacher preparation. This elevated approach to preparing congregants to teach helps Christian education programs rise to the challenge of today's church.

Appreciation

This book could not have been completed without the support of my brothers and sisters who have encouraged me to press beyond my limits: Frank, Linda Joyce, Linda Faye, Johanna, and Parish. I am especially grateful to Terrence Hargrove, who would not let me quit until this work was done. I appreciate the many people who have encouraged this work through their positive feedback in the workshops and classes I have taught. I thank Juliana Stratton and Kimberlee Burt for helping me view Christian education and children's ministry from a fresh perspective.

I am grateful to Alice Large, Dr. Dale Johnson, Anita Cotton, and Bernadine Jackson, whose vision and passion for Christian education has never waned.

I thank my instructors at National-Louis University and McCormick Theological Seminary for reinforcing my desire to see quality teacher preparation in all areas of life.

I appreciate the daughters and sons God has placed in my life; they have blessed me beyond measure. I thank God for the women and men who have prayed for me and walked this journey with me as co-laborers in Christ.

To all who have contributed to the completion of this book by sharing your gift in publishing or your voice in prayer—I thank you.

SECTION ONE

Elevate: The Need to Change Perspectives

You are the salt of the earth. But what good is salt if it has lost its flavor? Can you make it salty again? It will be thrown out and trampled underfoot as worthless. You are the light of the world—like a city on a hilltop that cannot be hidden. No one lights a lamp and then puts it under a basket. Instead, a lamp is placed on a stand, where it gives light to everyone in the house. In the same way, let your good deeds shine out for all to see, so that everyone will praise your heavenly Father. Matthew 5:13–16, NIV

And so, dear brothers and sisters, I plead with you to give your bodies to God because of all he has done for you. Let them be a living and holy sacrifice—the kind he will find acceptable. This is truly the way to worship him. Don't copy the behavior and customs of this world, but let God transform you into a new person by changing the way you think. Then you will learn to know God's will for you, which is good and pleasing and perfect. Romans 12:1–2, NIV

Can We Answer God's Call?
God calls the church to reach the world with the Gospel, to be salt and light, to be worshipers who strive to do God's will. The early church instinctively answered that call, and on the day of Pentecost, three thousand were baptized and added to the church (Acts 2:41). With that as a bar, the task to reach the world seems easy. The realization of how many people are in the world, and how many language and cultural barriers there are to getting the task done, makes it seem overwhelming. Competing faith traditions, denominations, and religions have left generations of confused seekers. Congregations are confronted by doubters suspicious of what the church has to offer in a digital world where reality television competes with virtual friendships to take minds off personal struggles. When the myriad of commitments placed on personal time and resources is factored in, reaching the world might seem impossible.

CHAPTER ONE

The Case for
Teaching in the Church

The Struggle We Face: Who Is in the Church?

Thinking about the difficulties of transmitting the Gospel in today's culture can lead one to accept the premise that the traditional church is losing ground.[3] After all, there has been a decrease in the population of mainline churches. Older persons have retained their commitment to and desire for traditional church attendance and relationships. The millennial generation has shied away from traditional worship centers and practices.[4] Nearly "59% of the young people who grow up in Christian churches end up walking away either from their faith or from the institutional church at some point in their first decade of adult life.... The unchurched segment among Millennials has increased in the last decade, from 44% to 52%, mirroring a larger cultural trend away from churchgoing among the nation's population."[5] On the other hand, many evangelical denominations are attracting new members. Pentecostal churches boast 500 million faithful making them the "second largest communion of Christians in the world (with potential) to reshape Christianity in the 21st Century."[6] These mixed messages of growth and decline leave some churches wondering how to be effective.

Church Attendance

The attendance struggle is not new. Diminishing church affiliation has been an issue for the past fifty years, yet "congregations continue to act as if their children will automatically take on the identity and mission of the church as adults."[7] One reason for this belief can be found in Deuteronomy 6, where parents are instructed to teach the precepts of the Law to their children so that the generations will continue in the faith. But families are no longer the conduit of spiritual development and nurture. Growing numbers of children do not live in homes with custodial parents. In 2011, over 400,000 children lived in foster care in the United States. Of that number 27% were in foster homes with relatives, but nearly 50% lived in nonrelative foster situations. Add to this the nine percent who were in institutions and the five percent who lived in group homes. That same year, there were more children emancipated from foster care than there were ten years earlier.[8] Only five years later (2016), the number children in foster care had grown to 437,465. Thirty-two percent of those children were in relatives' homes, but 45% were in nonrelative foster care. During that period over 250,000 children exited foster care, but 273,539 entered in that period.[9]

Changes in the pattern of church attendance and faith choices for adults imply that the family structure lacks the capacity to fully achieve the Deuteronomy 6 mandate for sharing the faith with children. "Fifty-nine percent of millennials who were brought up in the church have since dropped out."[10] When younger adults seek religious affiliation, it doesn't always mean a commitment to faith through the traditional church. The number of older adults claiming no religious affiliation accounts for 19.7% of the general population. This is a rise from the 8.1% in 1991. A 2008 Pew Study found that the decline in the Protestant population has been met with a significant increase in the number of people not affiliated with any particular religion.[11] By 2018, the Pew Research Center had determined that "one-third of the US adult population believes in a higher power of some kind, but not in God as described in the Bible."[12]

These data give only a partial picture of church attendance and faith beliefs. Statistics collected by religious organizations and research groups often exclude the masses of people who do not come from religious homes and have no exposure to church or church culture. Additionally, the worship patterns of minority populations are often excluded or underrepresented in these surveys.[13] There is also the growing appeal of non-Christian religions. The current trend toward spirituality apart from faith in Christ can make the quest to spread the Gospel seem insurmountable.[14]

Seeking Connections

Nevertheless, the human heart seeks God. People still look for spirituality to fill the void. Churches attempt to address the need by identifying new ways to fulfill the soul's quest. Their efforts, however, are not always successful. Mega-churches have set the pace for today's congregations who "look to the programmatic characteristics of the mega-church for clues about what their congregations should be doing."[15] Smaller churches often attempt to replicate the programs offered by these large congregations but find that those efforts do not result in the vitality of membership and resources they expect.

Technology has proven to be a useful tool for spreading the Gospel; but, churches must fully examine their efforts to incorporate the latest technologies in their programs and outreach efforts. Increasingly, online delivery systems provide worship and teaching to those who are either unable to or prefer not to attend church in person. The electronic church also has growing appeal for unaffiliated "worshipers" as well as prospective members and online donors. In fact, the digital church is fast becoming the norm. (Many pastors now think of membership in terms of traditional and online supporters.) But electronic approaches often attract those who are already Christians.[16] Attracting the unchurched is another issue. Yet, regardless of whether digital efforts target Christians or the unchurched, personal care and emotional wholeness can be lost in the digital mix. The *Wall Street Journal* reported a North Carolina church's plan to offer "virtual communion."[17] This minimalist approach to worship and Christian fellowship may provide a "bump" in attendance, but it can thwart efforts to develop deep faith by eroding confidence in the church.

Efforts to make the Gospel palatable to a new generation have led some ministries to avoid denominational labels. Given the draw of our pluralistic society, these churches are attempting to appear neutral in theology. This theological non-disclosure can result in marketing strategies that trivialize faith in Jesus Christ and encourage onlookers to seek God based on their religious "shopping preferences."[18] Having faith means more than just catching a spiritual ring in order to ride above life's emotional, social, and economic issues. When churches equate a name change with a spiritual "face lift," they may be doing a disservice as parishioners get the impression that theological perspective is, at best, tangential to faith. With that attitude, worshipers may respond like the seeds in Jesus' parable in Mark 4 that fell on stony ground and, without root, just withered away. Approaches to church attendance that are either cavalier or unproductive often cause seekers (and members) to think that faith in an omnipotent God is impossible and useless.

Church Membership and the Revolving Door

People change or leave churches for the same reasons people change residences. Older people move to housing that may be miles from their original home and church. Health issues can prevent continued attendance. Empty nesters are prone to downsizing to condos or senior communities that offer more activity with less stress than traditional home ownership. Parents seek churches that provide a wide range of programming for their children. Young adults are often called to other locations by work, marriage, or educational plans. These patterns are true in urban centers and rural areas. Members change congregations regardless of the size or location of the church.

These patterns leave churches in a quandary as well. Mainline denominations struggle to maintain members. Small churches ponder how to attract people to their doors. Yet mega-churches seem to grow effortlessly. They are often blamed for pushing a message of convenience and "stealing" members from other churches. Such accusations carry a trace of sour grapes. Because of their resources, mega-churches have a capacity for greater variety in programming. Their liturgy attracts diversity in membership. But mega-churches have troubles, too. They are often accused of failing to make real connections with members. In one study, three-quarters of the mega-churches studied grew by 10 percent or more. During that same period, however, twelve percent of them lost members.[19]

The term "revolving door" describes the tendency of church-goers to avoid long-term commitments to any local congregation. This pattern is not unique to any one denomination or type of church. In urban areas, for example, it is common for congregants to "church hop." Some people develop formal and informal bi-church memberships. They may have family loyalties to a "home church" but seek spiritual fulfillment in a "second church home" that may or may not be brick and mortar. These factors make it seem as if some people never really come out of the revolving door. Instead, they elect to "keep it moving" until the next time they drop by.

Lessons from 9-1-1

People flocked to churches the Sunday after September 11, 2001 because their spirits and hearts were broken by the collective tragedy our nation and the world experienced. Jesus' said, "Come unto me, all ye that labour and are heavy laden, and I will give you rest" (Matthew 11:28). This is an invitation not to religious pretense but to peace. The pain of 9-1-1- was real. The divine offer is authentic. A 2003 Gallup report found that immediately after September 11 there was "a spike in the percentage of Americans who reported attending church in the past seven days, from the generally stable level of 41% to 47%.... A similar effect was evident with respect to Americans' ratings of the importance of religion in their lives. This increased from 57% before the attack, to 64% shortly after."[20] However, a special report on The

PBS Program *Ethics and Religious Weekly* revisited responses to the 2001 attacks. The report found that the number of people who said religion was important to their lives returned to virtually the same level as in May 2001.[21] Obviously, many congregations were not up to the challenge of fulfilling the promise of hope.

Why Teaching Matters

Despite the problems of modern congregations, the local church continues to attract people. Charles Foster, Professor of Religion and Education at Emory University, finds that in the post-Christian era "congregations . . . are, in most communities, the only place where Christian values and perspectives are fully affirmed and communicated."[22] This means that despite the problems, the local church is standing strong as a counter-voice to the disparate clamor of society.

In order to effectively be that counter-voice, each local church must operate as a community of Spirit-led persons who are aware of the challenges people face today. Churches must be prepared to address real issues with biblical principles. The precedent for this is given in a conversation between Jesus and Peter. Following the Resurrection, Jesus questioned Peter's love and commitment three times while saying, "Feed my sheep" (John 21:15-17). Peter's actions on the day of Pentecost were his response to Jesus' demand. Peter instructed the masses by recounting their history, presenting their current dilemma, and challenging them to be reconciled to God through faith in Jesus Christ (Acts 2). Like Peter, today's church must confront its traditional and cultural worldview with a fresh understanding based on the Scriptures and the knowledge of Jesus as Messiah and Savior.

Following Peter's initial sermon, the crowd did not stand for the benediction and leave. Instead, they "continued stedfastly in the apostles' doctrine and fellowship, and in breaking of bread, and in prayers" (Acts 2:42). Why? They believed and were baptized, but they were compelled by the Holy Spirit to learn to walk in this new way of life through instruction, fellowship, and prayer. They followed Jesus' declaration: "Take my yoke upon you. Let me teach you..." (Matthew 11:29, NLT).

The church is the body of Christ, called to function cohesively in bringing people to the saving knowledge of Jesus Christ. The church has a responsibility to teach the Scriptures so that those who come to Christ can learn of Him. In order to do that, God has provided ministry gifts, spiritual in nature but practical in application. Teaching is not the only gift in the church, but it is critical to providing scriptural knowledge of Jesus Christ and His offer of salvation. The work of helping Christians mature is directed by the pastor or the ordained clergy assigned to the task. If local congregations are to operate effectively, they must give credence to the importance of teaching. To do this, churches must identify and equip congregational teachers to help seekers and believers grow in faith.

Paul's travels took him into communities that differed in worldviews. In each place, Paul preached and taught. The Holy Spirit added people to the church daily. A few people traveled with Paul, but the majority of people who responded to the message of the Gospel remained in their cities, towns, and villages. Sharing the Gospel requires that churches "go" to neighborhoods and cities. But it also means that those who reside in those places must participate fully in sharing the Gospel where they live. The church is the *ekklesia*, the ones called out to become members of the body of Christ. Yet believers remain members of cultural and social groupings. It is through teaching that congregations are prepared to share the Gospel within the cultural, socio-economic, and religious milieu of their communities.

All churches struggle with knowing whether congregants are developing spiritually. Churches that veer from the biblical model tend to reach for programmatic straws that may attract but not retain younger families and single adults.[23] Their helter-skelter path to spiritual growth calls into question claims to touch the surrounding neighborhoods. When congregations ignore the power of the Gospel they are unlikely to transform the lives of the people in the pews.

If local churches are to be effective in spreading the Gospel and strengthening people spiritually, they will need to reclaim the teaching ministry. In order to do that, teaching must be part of the congregational infrastructure. By retooling Christian education, congregational teachers can be equipped with biblical knowledge and skill sets that help local pastors and church leaders equip congregants of all ages. Congregational teachers are the human resource God has provided to the local church. Their involvement makes Christian education the rich vehicle for spiritual transformation it was intended to be.

Summary

Churches are rightly concerned about attracting people through the Gospel. Congregations are equally anxious about the spiritual formation and transformation of persons in their fellowships and those who are attracted by the Gospel. Regardless of how current trends and societal questions cast a shadow over those aims, the Bible provides solutions. Jesus Christ must be lifted as the One who draws all people to God (John 12:12). The Holy Spirit is the Comforter and Teacher who makes the difference (John 14:26; Acts 2:38).

The Bible provides clear examples of the important role teaching and learning have in developing people of faith. Jesus' ministry was teaching. The book of Acts carefully narrates the actions and results of the teaching done by the apostles. The epistles were written to teach new converts whose faith had been activated and lives transformed by the Holy Spirit (Acts 2:42). The New Testament teaches how the Old Testament foretold God's ultimate encounter with humanity through Jesus Christ, the expected Messiah and Living Word. The New Testament reveals God's eternal plan and the role of the Holy Spirit as Intercessor, Guide, and Teacher. The New Testament church was built by the ministry of teaching. Today's church must be maintained and propelled by it. The Bible is the connective tissue by which the church learns to live as the body of Christ. The teaching ministry, then, is the vocation to which we are called.

Consider:

1. This section begins with quotations from Matthew 5:13–16 and Romans 12:1–2. How do these passages relate to the chapter content?
2. This chapter has raised several issues regarding how churches may be spreading the Gospel, strengthening the spiritual lives of congregants, and engaging the gifts and talents of people. How would you describe these efforts in your congregation?
3. What membership trends have become evident in your neighborhood and congregation over the past five or ten years? Are any persons or people groups absent from either the community or the church? How are traditional and non-traditional families being reached?
4. The "revolving door syndrome" differs with each congregation. Can you identify it in your local assembly? What impact, if any, does it have on congregational life?
5. What are your congregation's core beliefs about teaching? Where and how are those beliefs manifested in your local assembly?

CHAPTER TWO

The State of Teaching Ministry

What's in a Name?

The terms "religious education" and "Christian education" are often used interchangeably. Some church leaders see religious education as an umbrella term for all teaching in the local church. That would make Christian education a subset of religious education. There are others, however, who see a broad chasm between the two.[24] Theologian Debra Dean Murphy argues that the intent of "religious education" is to teach religious tolerance and appreciation of *all* faith traditions. She explains that the early church was faced with a multiplicity of religious beliefs. The apostles, however, were not focused on helping new converts understand other religions. Their concern was helping those "called to be saints" to learn the person and nature of God as revealed in Jesus Christ (Romans 1:7).

Murphy's argument is a reminder that teaching in the context of the church is actually about a specific faith tradition. Christian education aims to help people journey into the practices of faith that are centered in Jesus Christ as Lord and Savior. Its primary objective is spiritual transformation, the change from "the old" self (Ephesians 4:22) to a "new creation" (2 Corinthians 5:17). Christian education demands a worldview that is anchored in Christianity. It cannot occur within the synagogues of Judaism or the mosques of Islam. It can occur outside the walls of the church but not outside the fiber of its faith. Christian education is based in Christ. Its story is revealed in the Bible. Its impact is catalogued through the teachings of the church and the chronicles of Christian community. The objectives of all Christian education endeavors must be uniquely Christian.

Yet, Christian education as conducted by non-clergy in local churches struggles to be effective. Why? The exploration of this view focuses on three factors: (1) The image of Christian education and its content, (2) Modern attitudes about those who provide Christian education ministry, and (3) The value given to Christian education as part of the life of the local church.

Christian Education: Tainted by Its History

Despite the Church's mandate to teach, Christian education as conducted by non-clergy in local churches struggles to be effective. Why? Because the image of Christian education today is tainted by its history and stifled by our attitudes. In order to elevate and revitalize Christian education, we must recognize how it is valued or devalued as part of the life of the local church.

The Blessing and Curse of Sunday School and VBS

Christian education in Protestant churches is often associated with Sunday school. Other names such as church school are used to broaden the concept, but Sunday school remains the core. It exists across denominations and represents a major focus of congregational teaching performed by non-clergy. When Robert Raikes started the Sunday school movement in England in the mid-1800s, it was revolutionary. His desire was to teach literacy and Anglican catechism to a generation of children who were forced to work in the sweatshops of England. Sunday school in the United States began with a similar aim. When compulsory education in the United States became law, it was no longer necessary to teach children to read and write on

Sundays. However, the popularity of Sunday school remained because of its focus on biblical instruction.[25] Since then, church services and Sunday school have been complementary activities in the flow of Sunday worship.

For over one hundred years, Sunday school was viewed as a rite of passage for children. Parents often sent children to local Sunday schools even when they did not attend themselves. "The trend for permissive parenting in the 1960s, however, meant that a widespread culture of insisting that children go to Sunday school . . . was abandoned."[26] Today, grandparents have often assumed the responsibility of taking grandchildren to Sunday school when their own children's efforts were lacking.

Despite the rumors, Sunday school still has some life in it. "Every weekend more than 300,000 churches offer some type of systematic religious instruction in a classroom setting…. Those programs are attended by nearly 45 million adults and more than 22 million youth and children."[27] Testimonies of spiritual formation and Christian heritage still position Sunday school as the flagship of Christian education. Today, most Sunday schools provide classes for all ages—from toddlers to the elderly. Yet the majority of Sunday school attendees are adults who experienced it as children.

Sunday school is often seen as the "face" of Christian education. The concept, however, has been adopted by another Christian education program: Vacation Bible School (VBS). One commercial publisher describes VBS as "[t]he premiere outreach event of the year for many churches."[28] VBS has traditionally served as a summer outreach to community youth and provides the same foundational Bible "stories" of faith as Sunday school. The history of Vacation Bible School can be traced to "the 1870s when the Methodist Episcopal Church offered summer Sunday school institutes to the general public near Lake Chautauqua, New York."[29] By 1873, churches were offering summer retreats and special services for children. In 1898 on "New York City's East Side Mrs. Walker Aylette Hawes of the Epiphany Baptist Church" held a VBS gathering.[30] Her concern was for the "increase in the number of immigrant children in the slums. Her program incorporated "worship music, Bible stories and Scripture memorization, games, crafts, drawing, cooking, etc."[31] In 1903, "Dr. Robert Boville, who worked for the Baptist Mission . . . (had) opened VBS in Philadelphia and Chicago."[32] By 1911, Boville had established national and international VBS boards.

As it gained prominence across the country, VBS became a two-week endeavor. Some churches still provide two weeks of VBS, but most Christian publishers of VBS materials only offer a one-week curriculum. Some churches focus their VBS efforts solely on children. Others offer VBS on week nights to attract families. VBS, however, has fallen victim to the pace of today's lifestyles. Operating costs have become a major problem as the general economy has caused congregational dollars to dwindle. In addition, parents prefer summer camps that focus on academic and athletic enrichment. With more mothers in the workforce, churches have seen a decline in the number of volunteers available to help. Working parents look for full-day options that also meet the need for childcare. The increasing demand on church and personal schedules accounts for a significant decline in the percentage of churches offering VBS.

Historically, Sunday school and VBS were able to attract parents to local churches through the engagement of their children. That has shifted. Today's parents are looking for churches that offer a wide menu of programs for the entire family. Churches, while they accommodate children fully, are just as concerned with attracting adults—with or without children—who will be committed and engaged in worship and other activities in the congregation. It is no wonder then that many churches view Sunday school and VBS as out-of-sync efforts that are unable to keep pace with the needs of new generations.[33]

The Issue of Curriculum

Nevertheless, Sunday school manages to remain at the forefront of Christian education. The main reason is its curriculum.

On any given week, individuals in churches across the country are all focusing on the same Scripture lessons. This "International Lesson" concept is the brainchild of the National Council of Churches (NCC). A 2002 article calls this "a remarkable, 130-year exercise in Christian unity (that) quietly undergirds the church school lessons millions use every week." Also known as "The Uniform Lesson Series," these curricular outlines provide a six-year scope and sequence of Bible study for children, youth, and adults. These NCC frameworks are developed by Christian educators from various communions, denominations, and publishing houses. They are then purchased by independent and denominational publishers who develop and sell curricula.[34]

The development of Sunday school curricula has become a lucrative and influential industry. Historically, independent Christian publishers such as Gospel Light, Standard Publishing, Union Gospel Press, David C. Cook, and Urban Ministries promoted the importance of organized curriculum as a vehicle for biblical literacy. While acquisitions have now narrowed the number of independent companies, there is still a market looking for and depending on published materials.[35] These structured and age-appropriate curricular resources strive to be both teacher-friendly and teacher-proof. Volunteers with little biblical or teaching background can use them. They also leave room for creative teachers to use their knowledge of the Bible and the needs of their classes to customize lessons.

Each publishing house attempts to create a niche market within the industry. Two independent publishers appeal directly to the cultural dynamic. Urban Ministries Inc., "the largest independent, African American-owned and operated Christian media company" was developed to address the void of African American images, history, and cultural perspectives in published Sunday school materials.[36] David C. Cook, whose primary target is mainstream churches, offers their Sunday school curriculum with graphics as well as historic information that specifically targets African American and Hispanic cultures.

Competition for Christian education curricular dollars also follows denominational lines. A 2005 study revealed that 52% of the churches surveyed use curricular materials designed by their denominations.[37] Presbyterian, Methodist, American Baptist, and Southern Baptist leadership have developed their own materials with denominational distinctives and branding.[38] Two large African American Baptist denominations have long-standing publications. R.H. Boyd is an independent publisher whose history and affiliations are in the National Baptist Church-America. The Sunday School Publishing Board is operated by the National Baptist Convention, USA Inc. Some denominations turn to independent Christian publishers who then "imprint" resources by putting a denominational label on their commercial materials. In a few cases, the companies collaborate with denominational educators to create customized materials that would otherwise be beyond the denomination's capacity to produce.

Regardless of the source of the materials, many of these resources focus their efforts on children. Familiar narratives such as Daniel and the Lion's Den or the birth of Jesus are repeated within the cycle usually according to the liturgical calendar. As a result, many people equate Sunday school with "children's stories," giving the impression that Sunday school resources lack theological depth. To combat the view that Christian education materials are inferior for adult study, publishers have upgraded the educational value of their materials. They rely on research on teaching and learning to develop lesson plans. Commercial publishers and denominations also offer training designed to increase teacher knowledge and assure the best use of their materials.

The Sunday school model of Christian education and the dependence on commercial curricula have eroded the idea that congregational teaching is a *ministry* that can adequately impact the entire church. By allowing a paradigm of consumerism to dominate the vision of Christian education, congregations have abdicated their responsibility to craft teaching in the church. This is not an appeal to abandon commercial or denominational Sunday school materials. Published curricula are valuable. However, churches must not forego their responsibility to determine how and when these materials are really aiding their efforts to teach for spiritual maturity.

Attitudes Regarding Christian Education Today

Christian education has historically been a major part of congregational life. Today, however, the local church seems to struggle more than ever with how to position Christian Education as an effective ministry of the church. It is linked to the "schooling model of modern pedagogy with its emphasis on classrooms, instruction, teaching techniques, theories of human development, and the designing and implementing of curricula."[39] Christian education seeks to influence the spiritual lives of believers, but is often seen as existing outside the framework of church life. This "perpetuates the false divide between worship and Christian formation."[40] The result is the "othering" of Christian education as a phenomenon that mimics secular instruction but lacks the power needed for spiritual transformation. At the root of the problem are three issues: education, volunteerism, and bias.

An (Un)Educated Leadership

Churches that can afford it, hire ordained clergy who have adequate college and seminary backgrounds to design and conduct Christian education experiences for the congregation. However, in many Pentecostal and charismatic churches, graduation from recognized, accredited institutions is not the norm even for the pastor. In fact, ordination may not require any theological or biblical instruction as formal education takes a back seat to spiritual experience and "the call."

High school and college graduation rates for individuals who grow up in charismatic and Pentecostal churches are far less than the national norms.[41] This does not mean that these leaders and church educators do not want to learn to better address congregational concerns. Educational opportunities, when they are sought, are generally found in unaccredited schools that espouse the tenets of that faith tradition. Individuals, therefore, turn to these pseudo-educational venues hoping to increase their preparedness for ministry. Unfortunately, "of the approximately 150 Pentecostal and charismatic 'institutions of higher education' . . . only 26 (17%) hold regional accreditation."[42] The result is a generation of under-educated church leaders and Christian educators who struggle to craft quality programs that are able to spark spiritual transformation. Although they feel called to lead churches and educational programs, these leaders often lack adequate ministry and administrative skills to organize instruction that addresses issues of faith development.

The Volunteer Pool

Because churches lack both financial and human resources, they must recruit volunteers to serve in Christian education. There are several problems connected to the volunteer option. First, volunteerism in the church and society is low. The shrinking volunteer pool results in large part from the pressure people are under from work, home, and family responsibilities. "An estimated 21% of households in the United States are impacted by caregiving responsibilities.... Eighty-three percent of these people are unpaid persons such as family members, friends, and neighbors of all ages who are providing care for a relative."[43] In addition, more people are struggling to make ends meet. According to the Bureau of Labor Statistics, despite a better outlook than in 2011, 10.5% of families in 2012 included an unemployed person.[44] From 2000 to 2012, real US median household income decreased 6.6%. By 2012, people who worked multiple jobs during the week were also twice as likely to work weekends as people who held only one job.[45] Although the May 2018 unemployment rate has dropped to 3.9%, "long-term unemployed (those jobless for 27 weeks or more) was little changed . . . and accounted for 20.0 percent of the unemployed."[46] Regardless of the drop in unemployment, the average person is still struggling to make ends meet. Given these data it is not difficult to understand the problem of making additional time commitments.

Even when churches can secure volunteers, they find it difficult to identify "an adequate core of persons with the vision, training, and experience to sustain educational ministries capable of creating a faithful and viable future for congregational life."[47] Too many local churches end up accepting any well-intentioned candidate who is willing to help. These volunteers may have the zeal to work but may not be aware of the biblical and theological knowledge congregational teaching requires. This has led to drastic and negative repercussions. Congregations have accepted into the ranks of "teacher" people who are relatively new to the faith. They have recruited people with little or no knowledge of the Bible. Some churches have allowed anyone who can pass the background check to work with the children.

Perhaps these actions account—at least partially—for the skeptical way in which volunteers are viewed. Because churches have a different expectation of paid staff and volunteers, they have unconsciously celebrated one while tolerating the other. As a religious educator, Maria Harris' concern for the term laity seems to summarize the problem. As a church staffer, she saw the division of clergy and laity as symbolizing a have-and-have-not relationship. Harris felt that the divide denied the "often complementary . . . and overlapping" roles required to live out our calling as members of the body of Christ.[48] Michelle Van Loon points out that the use of the terms such as "volunteers," "laity," or "unordained" often devalue the contribution of those who serve as congregational teachers.[49]

> When we viewed fellow congregants as volunteers, we subtly emphasized what they could do over against who they were as members of the body of Christ. I wondered if we were unintentionally building a culture where 'our volunteers' were our blue-collar laborers, doing tasks assigned by us, the white-collar staff.[50]

When people do accept volunteer positions in Christian education, many are not highly prepared for the task. They represent a broad spectrum of skills and gifts. The range of teaching abilities in the church (as in secular education) includes both remarkable teachers and persons who are "in the army of the Lord" but ill-equipped for the task. For every outstanding teacher, congregations have two or more people who struggle to teach effectively. To overcome this, churches provide training in the form of one or more orientation sessions. Some congregations utilize the workshops offered by denominations or commercial publishers for help. The majority of this preparation focuses on skill training for presenting curricular information. Some sessions may mention age-level characteristics of learners or strategies for personal Bible study. Little else is explored.

While these are helpful and often excellent short-term events, they are inadequate preparation for the teaching ministry. They do not include the critical thinking, reflection, and discourse needed to elevate teacher knowledge, skills, and spiritual dispositions. Churches must be careful to value the teaching process and the persons who participate in the work of Christian education. They must give thought to how they will incorporate members of the congregation into the work of the church. How churches address the need to prepare teachers is an indication of the value church leaders place on the ministry of teaching for transformative change.

Unconscious Bias

Traditional Sunday school practices have contributed to this marginalized view of Christian Education. While some churches have made changes, traditional Easter programs still bring children into the sanctuary to recite speeches and act out "Bible stories." The children are then ushered back to the "children's corner." By the time these young people are teens, they have learned to devalue the contribution of the teaching ministry to their lives and congregational life. As a result, they find ways to either avoid the classes or to act out their discontent when they are forced to be present.

Language is another evidence of the othering of Christian education. Labeling the work of church members as "*only* teaching Sunday school" or "*just overseeing* Children's church" devalues their contribution. Their efforts are then viewed as non-critical to the work of the church. Statements like "we leave church school" to "go to church" infer that there is a great chasm to cross in order to enter His courts with praise. Descriptions that link Christian education as events that occur "before" or "after" worship imply that these experiences have a different (or no) significance in the life of congregants. Teaching time cannot be less valued than worship time. It definitely cannot be viewed as irrelevant to the worship experience.

Finally, the teaching ministry provides opportunities for encounters with God through Scripture study; therefore, the act of teaching the Word of God should render the space where teaching occurs as hallowed ground. Think about Moses on Mount Horeb (Exodus 3). Nothing about the mountain or the bush was very significant until Moses was led there to experience God's presence. What started as curiosity turned to awe when God spoke.

A space is considered sacred when the activities that occur there anticipate sacred encounters with God. The issue of sacred space for Christian education calls into question the attitudes with which church leaders and planners prepare for instruction. Honoring the space set aside for Christian education as holy ground requires a change in how those spaces are arranged to facilitate that purpose. Keeping the space sacred means that having chairs available should not be an after-thought. It means not switching the meeting area on a whim. It means giving teachers advanced notice of changes that will affect their classes and learners' experiences. It means respecting what happens in that space by not interrupting the flow of the lesson with preemptive activities that ignore the instructional effort. It means that when churches set aside time for Christian education they must honor that time as part of the worship experience.

Summary

Our present vision of Sunday school, and other Christian education practices and traditions, confirms the need for a new approach to teacher preparation and the teaching ministry. The blessing and curse of traditional programs such as Sunday school and Vacation Bible School have shaped teaching in the local church. For many younger worshipers, the history of Christian education is not known, but the influence of its history remains. As a result, congregations have too often failed to give sufficient support to the programs and persons that are part of the teaching ministry either because they didn't know what support to provide or they undervalued the role of these activities and church members. When the need for teacher preparation is ignored, churches neglect the development of the gifts people bring to the Christian education table. The result is a minimization of teaching as a ministry. This lessens the effectiveness of the local church's collective witness and mission. Failure to examine practices and attitudes about Christian education and those who teach dishonors the work and the members who serve in that capacity.

When churches value the work of Christian education and the places where this work occurs, they show that they also value the people engaged in these educational encounters. Christian education aims to help congregants live in the newness of life as Christians. The question of who can and should operate as teachers in the church is nuanced by the way we view clergy, laity and volunteers. Changes in our lifestyles and the pressures of work and family have changed our view of the value of congregational teaching and our availability to do the work. When Christian education is viewed as tangential to the church's program or secondary to worship experiences, the teaching, the people, and the place become peripheral as well. Local churches can re-vision the importance of the teaching ministry by valuing its teaching and learning encounters as part of the worship and transformation experiences of the church.

Consider:

1. In your church or faith tradition, how is the teaching ministry organized?
2. Who are the persons responsible for congregational teaching in your church?
3. Besides the sanctuary, what places are sacred in your church? What makes those places "sacred spaces?"
4. Prepare to interview someone who teaches in your congregation. Ask if published curriculum is part of the preparation and presentation of lessons. How helpful are those materials?
5. Engage others in the discussion based on one or more of the points raised in this chapter.

CHAPTER THREE

The Divine Nature of Congregational Teaching

God in the Center

Congregational teaching has both a pedagogical purpose and a divine nature. Its theological framework comes from the scriptural record of God's interactions with humanity. When congregational instruction fails to place God at the center of the educational pursuit, spiritual transformation is no longer the object of the endeavor. The principles and purpose of teaching for faith are divinely inspired. When teacher preparation programs unpack these doctrines, teachers and the congregation better understand the role of teaching in God's plan for the church. The issue is whether congregations intentionally engage Bible teaching the way the Bible proposes. *Elevate the CORE* calls for a Bible-centered approach to congregational teaching in order to evoke spiritual transformation.

Ministry as Service

The word "ministry" is most commonly used to describe the work of ordained clergy. Ordination carries a heightened responsibility to the body of Christ. The ordained person is expected to serve congregants and walk with them through life experiences ranging from birth to death. Government agencies in most states have given ordained clergy status as "mandated reporters." They expect the ordained person to serve the community by appealing to civil law for the protection of children and others.

In the Old Testament, several Hebrew terms are translated as this English word "ministry." Each refers to service and is characterized by actions that occur in worshiping God. In Numbers 4:12, the word "shareth" denotes the servile work of the priests in tending to the materials used in service of the Temple during Israel's offerings to the Lord. In 2 Chronicles 7:6, the Hebrew word *yad*, which means praise, is translated as ministry. It describes the service of the Levites, who played instruments in praise of God during the dedication of Solomon's Temple. Hosea 12:10 (NLT) uses the word *yad* to refer to the ministry of the prophets who served God by giving "visions and parables" to Israel so they might render honor and praise to God. The Old Testament understanding of ministry then is the service conducted by the priests in guiding the sacrifice.

In the New Testament, the word translated as ministry is *diakonia*. It refers to the area of work one does in service to faith. The ability to minister is an act of the Holy Spirit. Likewise, serving is a response to the saving grace of God. It is the grace of God that has caused the Holy Spirit to reside in individual believers so that members of the faith community are positioned to serve the body. The sixth chapter of Acts points out the use of this term when the Hellenist widows complained that they were not being given adequate portions of food. The response by the apostles was that specific men should be selected to oversee this ministry. From this example we learn that the service provided as ministry to the body is for the good of all. It is to be undertaken by those appointed by leadership. The ministry is not something undertaken by one person but by many persons who collectively provide what the body needs to be sustained. In the Old Testament, we repeatedly read that the ministry was conducted by the priests. Peter explains in 1 Peter 2:5, 9 that all believers constitute the "holy" and "royal priesthood." Because the New Testament places all believers in the priesthood, all believers have a responsibility to serve God by ministering to others.

Teaching as Ministry

The Old Testament priests prepared animals for sacrificial offering. The New Testament records the transition from the Old Testament model to the New Testament priesthood, where the priest/believer is the sacrifice in praise for the grace God freely gives (Romans 12:1). This change requires transformation. God has ordained a new order, a kingdom in which believers are admonished to "be not conformed to this world: but ye transformed by the renewing of your mind" (Romans 12:2).

It is the responsibility of the church and its communities of believers to "train people to be good and faithful citizens (of the kingdom of God)." The church, therefore, "has the responsibility for instructing people in the civics of the kingdom."[51] The epistles are concerned in part with instructing kingdom citizens in this new relationship. The writers use several metaphors for the instructional processes that nurture spiritual transformation. Peter refers to "the sincere milk of the word" that helps new converts "grow thereby" (1 Peter 2:2). Paul uses milk and meat as metaphors for teaching (1 Corinthians 3:2). Throughout the epistles, teaching in the context of the congregation is anchored in Old Testament Scriptures. Teaching, therefore, must challenge the theological understanding of kingdom citizens. Their transformation is connected to their knowledge of Christ (Ephesians 4:13) and the history of faith in God through the Scriptures.

While the Holy Spirit is the agent for change, those who teach in the congregation must recognize that their teaching is in service of their faith in Christ. The teaching ministry requires these servants to know the Bible. They must be able to declare to the congregation who God is. For congregational teaching to be effective, church education programs must "introduce lay leaders to theological reflection on biblical texts." Without this preparation, lay teachers "are confined to their own opinions and interpretations" and congregational teaching is diminished.[52] Spiritual transformation calls for Christians to reassess their actions, thoughts, and interactions based on their new position in Christ as kingdom citizens and children of God. Teaching for transformation requires that instruction be provided as ministry or service to the church that is aided and propelled by faith in God.

The Gift to Teach

The Holy Spirit enables individual believers to be of specific service to the body of Christ. Paul names teaching as a gift that, like all gifts, is given according to God's grace (Romans 12:6-7). Teaching is one of the gifts that helps in "perfecting of the saints, for the work of the ministry, for the edifying of the body of Christ" (Ephesians 4:12). The spiritual gift of teaching enables congregants to exercise the responsibilities and duties of teaching. This is seen in the New Testament when "ordinary people" such as Philip, Priscilla, and Aquila teach on a personal level with wisdom and power as they are led by the Holy Spirit (Acts 8, 18).

The spiritual gifts, however, must be encouraged, prepared, and used. Paul admonishes Timothy to "stir up the gift of God" (2 Timothy 1:6). This mandate to rekindle or fan the flames of one's gift referred to the authority and sanction ceremonially bestowed upon Timothy by Paul. Paul's message to Timothy presents a major principle for Christian education leaders. They must execute their responsibility to help individual members recognize and "stir up" the gifts that have been bestowed on them by the Holy Spirit. If all members of the body are to contribute to the life and work of the church, then all members must be prepared to undertake the responsibility of executing their gifts.

The Holy Spirit gives the *gift of teaching* to the body of Christ, assuring that teaching will be perpetual so that all members may engage in sharing the Gospel message. It is this gift of teaching, empowered by the Holy Spirit and based in the Scriptures, that provides the infrastructure for the sustenance of new life among believers. The gift of teaching is embedded in the fiber of the church. It helps to create the tapestry by which the church is known.

Teaching in the context of the church must encompass the "entire course of the church's life."[53] The key to Christian learning is worship with its accompanying practices of faith: proclamation, community, and service.[54] It is within the explicit and implicit curricular work of the church that Christian education takes place. Every aspect of church life and culture proclaim its theological foundation—its declaration of who God is. The gift of teaching is bestowed by the Holy Spirit on the church for corporate understanding of God's Word.

The Call to Teach

Teaching is a ministry to the body of Christ and a gift to the church. There is also a call to teach. This call is both corporate and personal. Recognizing the call of the local church to the ministry of teaching begins with the recognition of the divine nature of the endeavor. The Holy Spirit calls us to salvation through faith in the death, burial, and resurrection of Jesus Christ. Our acceptance of that invitation of grace provides the undeniable call to serve the body of Christ according to God's divine will. Our placement as believers *in* the body of Christ is a gift of God *to* the body. God's gift to the believer is the opportunity to fulfill the ministry or service to which we are individually and collaboratively called.

Paul's ministry exemplifies the call to teach. He recognized that living in the new kingdom and appropriately using the gifts God has given to the church required instruction. Enabled by the Holy Spirit, Paul's epistles were his vehicles for teaching. His aim was to help converts live in the newness of this gift of grace. He sought to help them exercise the gifts given by God for the work of the ministry of transformation (Romans 12).

David Bartlett, writing in *Paul's Vision for the Teaching Church*, expounds on Paul's theological foundation for the teaching ministry: "For Paul, teaching is not just a matter of passing on information but of evoking faithful obedience . . . the church's teaching is not just a matter of giving people new ideas but a matter of giving them new life, of setting them free from sin, and of putting them in a right relationship to God and to other people."[55] Paul as well as the other apostles and believers named in various books of the New Testament operated in the ministry of teaching as a call on their lives to serve the body of Christ.

Summary

Ephesians 4:11–12 explains the purpose of the gifts operating through various persons within the church, including teachers. The divine gifts are "[f]or the perfecting of the saints, for the work of the ministry, for the *edifying* of the body of Christ." The question posed in this book is whether the call and gift of teaching are valued equally with the call and gifts in other areas of the church. If the body metaphor of 1 Corinthians 12 is correct, then we must ask where the teaching ministry fits in serving God and the congregation. If churches understand the need to help converts in their journey of transformation, they will fully embrace teaching as a ministry gift that can edify (build up, strengthen) the body of Christ.[56]

Christian education departments must fully embrace and celebrate that which God has ordained for the benefit of the church. Christian education leaders must invest in preparing teachers to undergird the pastoral ministry and give comfort and clarity to those who partake of the milk and meat of the Gospel. The call and gift of teaching should compel the local church to re-define, re-instate, and celebrate the ministry of teaching as a viable and life-giving work of the church so that the church can operate according to God's "good, and acceptable, and perfect, will" (Romans 12:2).

Consider:

1. In what way is God in the center of your congregation's Christian education work?
2. In your own words, define ministry. Explain whether you see teaching as a ministry to the church. In the local assembly.
3. What spiritual gifts do you possess that enable you to serve the church? How were your gifts encouraged and by whom?
4. In what area of service has God called you to minister? Why do you consider this a call? How is, or was, your call nurtured?
5. How does the Christian education program in your church help teachers discern whether they are called to teach?
6. How is the gift of teaching evident in your congregation?

SECTION TWO

Foundations: The Catalysts of Transformation

Go ye therefore, and teach all nations, baptizing them in the name of the Father, and of the Son, and of the Holy Ghost: Teaching them to observe all things whatsoever I have commanded you: and, lo, I am with you always, even unto the end of the world. Amen. (Matthew 28:19-20)

Those things, which ye have both learned, and received, and heard, and seen in me, do: and the God of peace shall be with you. (Philippians 4:9)

The Three Dimensions of Congregational Teaching

Effective teaching employs both art and science in its effort to maximize how people learn. As a scientific endeavor, teaching employs strategies that can be learned and refined with practice. Skillful teaching can be scientifically observed, studied, and described. The science of teaching identifies learning objectives or targets by which teachers organize and coordinate the interaction of content, activities, and materials that are employed in the lesson and assessed through formal tests or informal observations. The art of teaching involves instinct and imagination. It intuitively guides student response. The artistry of teaching involves performance and style. The ability to make smooth transitions or address unexpected turns in the lesson further demonstrates its artistry. Artful teaching is engaging and relevant to learners. Because it melds science and art, teaching has the power to impact memory and action.

Congregational teaching has a third dimension. Richard Osmer, in *Teaching for Faith*, writes that the efforts of the teacher must "create a context in which faith can be awakened, supported and challenged."[57] In addition to the employ of art and science, congregational teaching anticipates and plans lessons that call

43

learners to faith. In John 14, Jesus said, "…The Advocate, the Holy Spirit, whom the Father will send in my name, will teach you all things and will remind you of everything I have said to you" (John 14:26, NIV).

Congregational teaching expects and relies on the presence of the Holy Spirit as part of the teaching-learning experience. It is this spiritual dynamic that moves congregational teaching from conveying information to transforming faith.

Teachers do not know everything participants are experiencing, but the Holy Spirit does. The Spirit connects learners' memories and situations in ways that render lessons critical and relevant to students' lives. Christian educators who are diligent about engaging the Spirit's presence are prayerful about approaching this endeavor. They are mindful of how they engage the art and science of teaching. Their prayers are honest petitions for the Holy Spirit to meet learners' needs, guide the teacher, and enable spiritual insight. When the Holy Spirit acts upon and through the teaching and learning process, the catalysts that undergird congregational teaching create emotional, psychological, and spiritual meaning. Teachers must be prepared to teach knowing that the Holy Spirit provides the power to transform.

Transformation is the end-game of congregational teaching. Chapter four identifies the five features that give evidence of transformative learning. Chapters five through eight identify each of the four pillars of effective congregational teaching.

The Five Features: Essentials of Christian Learning

Examining the Five Features of Transformative Learning

The effectiveness of congregational teaching can be identified through five features: knowledge, skill, attitude, spiritual disposition, and behavior. Because teaching aims to address student knowledge, skill, and behavior, it can also change attitudes. Congregational teaching, however, is intentional in its effort to impact spiritual dispositions. These features represent neither a sequential checklist nor a hierarchy of actions. Their relationship is fluid. The acquisition of knowledge may yield a change in attitude before being evident in specific behaviors or skills. Regardless of how these features are manifested, they constitute the focus of congregational teaching and spiritual transformation.

Feature 1: Knowledge

The acquisition of biblical knowledge means more than just being biblically literate. Teaching must lead to more than Scripture memorization and drills of Bible facts. Knowledge of the Scriptures means familiarity with Bible verses as well as the narratives and circumstances behind those passages. While specific content will vary with the age of the students, knowing the first audience, purpose, history, author, style, and other considerations of the text helps learners understand the tenets of the faith through the history and theology of the Bible. In this way, the Bible becomes more than a series of "stories" that are examined and re-examined through church classes. Based on age-appropriate instruction, learners must understand the biblical text and not just mimic what it has come to mean (or has been assumed to mean) over time. Not every learner needs to become a Bible scholar. The Bible, however, must be understood so that it becomes the mirror with which individuals examine their lives (James 1:22–25) and the compass for believers' spiritual journeys (Psalm 119:105).

A learner's prior knowledge about a topic, experiences with matters of faith, and personal circumstance can impact the acquisition of knowledge. The teacher's efforts, therefore, must focus on helping students recognize the Bible's relevance. When this occurs, the Bible "confronts earth with heaven and brings eternity to bear upon time."[58] Let's say a church exists in an area where the local plant has just dismissed a number of workers. The economic concern is a critical context because it is a shared experience that is uppermost in learners' minds. Despite the importance of the event, the plant closing cannot be the sole topic of the lesson. Doing that would likely fuel additional anger, frustration, and fear. Giving preference to the situation minimizes the biblical content and renders the Scriptures irrelevant. Learners are left to focus on solutions based on their emotional and financial dilemmas. No matter how excellent the discussion, nothing will elevate the conversation beyond the drudgery and pain of the current situation. As a result, the teaching encounter will be anchored in an earth-bound topic. The lesson will forfeit its ability to spiritually transform lives and console wounded persons.

The plant closing, therefore, must be considered from the perspective of students' spiritual journeys. This does not mean that the issue should be super-spiritualized. "God will make a way somehow" is true. The lesson, however, must point students to the knowledge of how the eternal God has been making a way all along—and will continue to do so. The plant closing has to be acknowledged, but the teacher must be prepared to help the class examine the situation through a lens of Scripture, faith, tradition, and experience.[59]

Congregants will ask how God could allow the plant to close when their livelihoods are at stake. Questions like this do not doubt God or faith. They provide an opportunity for teachers to help learners address "the difficult business of being Christian in the fray of the real world."[60] Teachers need to infuse the promises of God into the discussion so that learners can recall how they have personally experienced the fulfillment of God's promises in the past. As participants discuss the spiritual disciplines that have sustained them in previous times of despair, their testimonies give strength even to the newest Christians. The actions of one lesson will not put all concerns to rest, but as fears are allayed, class members are strengthened by the knowledge that God will never leave them nor forsake them. When congregational lessons bolster faith, student knowledge of God increases and the Bible becomes the fulcrum in balancing learners' experiences and personal trials. Teaching is transformative when knowledge is generated in light of learners' spiritual journeys.

Feature 2: Skill

At a retreat for Christian educators, participants discussed the importance of spiritual formation. One teacher was frustrated by the apathy of adults who were members of the faith community but complacent about their spiritual development. She finally asked, "Why can't we just say, 'Grow?'" Her solution would be a good one if transformation were that easy. Faith formation is spiritual and, thus, beyond human capacity alone. There is no human agency that can demand spiritual awakening or maturity. Yet, the teaching ministry aims to ignite and support the transformation process. For this, teachers must help learners acquire skill in engaging spiritual practices and employing their gifts and talents in ways that move students from spiritual milk to the meat of spiritual transformation (1 Corinthians 3:2; 1 Peter 2:2).

This requires teachers to help students develop confidence in their faith. To that end, the skill and practice needed to strengthen faith is like the skills and practice needed to ride a bicycle. Both processes require skill that builds confidence in balance and navigation. Regardless of the excitement children have about learning to ride, the fear of falling is not far away. Because getting balance is not always easy, children start with training wheels. They advance gradually with Mom or Dad holding them until they are finally going on their own. Balance is something they will know when they achieve it. It can only be truly understood when they stay upright for a period of time. If they get it once, they know what to expect the next time and will work even harder to gain the confidence to soar effortlessly through time and space again.

People who come to be baptized or enter into fellowship with a local assembly are generally excited. They have realized a life-decision and made a choice to live in a way they expect to be powerfully different from before. But this is not easy because life, like the concrete beneath that bicycle, is waiting. The new believer's fear of falling or of not pleasing God is real. For those who are just beginning their journey of faith, the teaching ministry serves that "training wheel" purpose. It provides the community that supports their journey. Competent and concerned teachers will help students develop the skill needed for establishing and exercising devotional practices and identifying biblical principles that will bring balance to their lives. Congregational teaching provides safe space where learners can ask questions and grapple with biblical texts as they identify their place in the faith community.

Faithful living requires skill. Students must be taught and encouraged to develop faith-centered practices as a way of life. Bible reading and prayer, meditation and fasting are important spiritual disciplines. Learners need to know the importance of Scripture study as part of the transformation process. When students develop skill in exercising spiritual disciplines, their faith is bolstered and they have an even greater appreciation for their new life in Christ.

Feature 3: Attitude

Attitude describes the way people carry themselves—whether with confidence or reticence. Attitude is shown in the outward responses of learners to people, situations, and circumstances. One aim of teaching for faith formation is to change and cultivate attitudes. Congregational teaching challenges learners to think differently about their lives and their choices in light of their relationship with God. In order to change attitudes, teachers must help learners develop a Bible-centered framework for making decisions.

In most situations, people determine their actions and choices based on their attitudes about the options available to them. For example, if someone is offended, he consciously or subconsciously considers his options before he responds. Option one might take into account the attitudes others have demonstrated in similar situations. A person may respond as she has seen family members, mentors, or peers react in the past. In option two, the person might consider his relationship with the offender. The attitude shown in approaching conflict with a co-worker may be very different from the attitude demonstrated during a conflict with an employer. A third option hinges on whether the offended person has confidence that someone will intervene on his behalf. Statements like, "Wait until my big brother comes," reveal confidence that a defender is on the way.

Transformative teaching aims to provide biblical, spiritual, and practical options for "attitude adjustment." The teaching ministry provides Bible-based principles that help learners reconsider how they respond to situations. Philippians 4:8 instructs believers to think about the things that are true, honest, just, pure, lovely, good, virtuous, and praiseworthy. These principles provide the catalysts learners need to resist dwelling on past injuries. Ephesians 5:19 advises Christians to speak to themselves "in psalms and hymns and spiritual songs, singing and making melody in your heart to the Lord." The take-away is a strategy for changing attitudes by controlling one's thoughts when painful memories or anger floods the mind. The knowledge gained through congregational teaching bolsters skill development and helps learners adjust their attitudes and re-evaluate their actions.

Feature 4: Spiritual Disposition

Spiritual disposition and attitude are similar, but they are not the same. Attitude involves the voluntary and often trained response to situations and stimuli. Changes in attitude can result from repeated mantras or mottoes that may have no spiritual basis. The decision to adjust an attitude can occur because someone reads a self-help book or sees a movie that resonates with him or her. Shakespeare's advice in *Hamlet* to "neither a borrower nor a lender be" is a sound recommendation for anyone.[61] If an individual makes up her mind to heed that advice, she will change her attitude about her financial decisions.

Spiritual disposition, on the other hand, is a God-given yearning for a deeper relationship with God. Jesus described spiritual disposition in Matthew 5:6 as our "hunger and thirst after righteousness," a desire that Jesus declared "shall be filled." Spiritual disposition, therefore, refers to the developing awareness of the value one places on spiritual matters. It is the affect that comes from the indwelling of the Holy Spirit. It is, therefore, anchored in spiritual rebirth (John 3:3-7). Spiritual disposition accounts for a heightened awareness of things holy.

> *What we have received is not the spirit of the world, but the Spirit who is from God, so that we may understand what God has freely given us . . . explaining spiritual realities with Spirit-taught words. The person without the Spirit does not accept the things that come from the Spirit of God but considers them foolishness, and cannot understand them because they are discerned only through the Spirit. (Excerpts from 1 Corinthians 2:12-14, NIV)*

Spiritual disposition is neither anchored in human relationships nor in personal frailties. It springs from one's acceptance of God's love through Jesus Christ.

When a person reads, hears, or realizes something that triggers the mind to understand a spiritual concept, the person will adjust his or her attitude. In the case of a spiritual disposition, the trigger is a spiritual revelation. It can come from reading a biblical text, hearing a sermon, or reflecting on an experience. The believer's faith in God is heightened as he or she embraces that spiritual concept. As spiritual disposition matures, faith is strengthened. This process is never-ending. The pinnacle of faith is never reached. One's spiritual disposition gets stronger as he or she matures in Christ through the study of the Bible. "For in the gospel the righteousness of God is revealed—a righteousness that is by faith from first to last, just as it is written: 'The righteous will live by faith'" (Romans 1:17).

In *The Craft of Teaching*, Israel Galindo asserts that the goal of all teaching lies in its intention to help learners become who God intended them to be.[62] Congregational teachers help students trust that there is a divine plan for each person (Jeremiah 29:11). As students embrace the concept of "becoming" their spiritual dispositions are acted upon by the Holy Spirit so that their understanding of life goes from transient to eternal. Teaching is a gift to the church. It is an agency through which the Holy Spirit operates on our inner-being to create spiritual awareness and openness to God. It is the Holy Spirit that develops spiritual dispositions that equip each believer for his or her unique spiritual journey.

Feature 5: Behaviors

Christian behaviors are actions that center on one's relationship with Jesus Christ as Lord and Savior. Identifying these behaviors should be an easy task. It is, however, complicated because faith communities often identify the behaviors that signify "Christian" to them based on their traditions, histories, and polity. How then can we determine the behaviors that indicate spiritual transformation and growth?

While denominations and communions may vary in their determination of which behaviors point to growing faith, the Bible provides clear direction in its admonition to exhibit those attitudes and behaviors that please God and do not grieve the Holy Spirit (Ephesians 4:30). While the entire Bible can be viewed as a "behavioral guide," the three Christian behaviors described in Romans 12 and 2 Corinthians 5 are foundational and directly relate to transformation. They are outward exhibits of an inner, spiritual change.

(1) Yield to God's Will – Romans 12:1 explains that believers should present their bodies as living sacrifices. The term "body" is a reference to our whole being—our physical, mental, emotional, and spiritual selves. One behavior that denotes spiritual transformation is the willingness to yield one's thoughts and desires to God. From the human standpoint, that is a huge deal! From the vantage point of Jesus Christ, who sacrificed Himself for us, submission is our reasonable service. The behavior then is evident in the believer's willingness to accept God's direction. Yielding is not easy. It calls even "the stuff" we thought was good into question as we employ a new compass for living. Yielding asks Christians to grapple through difficulties and sometimes question their understanding of faith. However, as believers read the Bible, practice spiritual discipline, and learn to trust God, they yield more willingly.

(2) Demonstrate a Spiritually Renewed Mind – In Romans 12:2 we read that we are no longer to be "conformed" to this world. Instead, we are to be "transformed by the renewing" of our minds. This renewal is the result of the indwelling Holy Spirit and acknowledges that the sacrifice of Jesus Christ was for the purpose of reconciling us to God, who "looked beyond our faults and saw our needs."[63]

The Amplified Bible refers to this renewal as a response to new ideals and attitudes. These renewed thoughts are indicators of the believer's spiritual disposition and transformative relationship with God. A spiritually renewed mind is demonstrated as a believer responds to times of joy, contentment, stress, pain, or failure by turning to God rather than turning to former modes of thought and action. The spiritually renewed mind strives to do the will of God and demonstrates actions that are indicative of a spiritual walk. They are the behaviors that demonstrate our efforts to do the "good, and acceptable, and perfect, will of God" as we respond to the challenges, successes, and even trivialities of life (Romans 12:2).

(3) Desire Reconciliation – Second Corinthians 5:17–18 reads,

> *If any man be in Christ, he is a new creature: old things are passed away; behold, all things are become new. And all things are of God, who hath reconciled us to himself by Jesus Christ, and hath given to us the ministry of reconciliation.*

One's behavioral change is noted in the embrace of the ministry of reconciliation, a process begun by God that results in a new "us." Transformation means first that our born-again selves are committed to reconciling our relationship with God. The realization that Jesus died for our sins brings the admission that we are unworthy of the forgiveness given to us through His sacrifice. In fact, we are powerless to "make it up" to God and must acknowledge that God grants us mercy when we fall short. Second, the ministry of reconciliation gives us the responsibility to share the Good News with others so that they, too, can find peace in God (2 Corinthians 5:18). Our spiritual dispositions aid our willingness and ability to share the Gospel through word and deed with those who don't know Christ (Romans 15:18). Finally, our desire for reconciliation is demonstrated in the way we mend our relationships with others (Romans 12:17–21).

Summary

Congregational teaching must aim to impact the five features of transformative learning: knowledge, skills, attitudes, spiritual dispositions, and behaviors. Each is governed by the student's knowledge of and relationship with Jesus Christ. Each represents an aspect of the learner's spiritual journey. Teachers who intentionally work toward transformative learning strive to promote a thirst in their students for spiritual development. They encourage students as they struggle and affirm learners in their spiritual walk. In order to determine how effective instruction is, teachers must observe how class encounters enhance students' biblical knowledge and devotional skills. Learners' attitudes, spiritual dispositions, and behaviors can change as the art and science of teaching is aided by the Holy Spirit to make a transformative difference.

Consider:

1. Think about a teacher who was special to you. What about his or her teaching demonstrated the science and art of teaching?
2. Congregational teaching can occur in gatherings outside the walls of the church. Can you identify three places outside the church premises where learning might occur? Explain how the five features might look in one of those places.
3. Reflect upon your personal spiritual journey. What changes in knowledge, skills, attitudes, spiritual dispositions, and behaviors have occurred in your faith walk? How? Now look forward. What changes do you still desire?
4. Several spiritual disciplines were described in this chapter. These included Bible reading, prayer, meditation, fasting. Consider also the disciplines of listening to sermons, listening to uplifting spiritual songs and hymns, and giving time to Scripture study. What disciplines would you add to this list? Which are evident in your devotional routine? What spiritual

disciplines intrigue you?

5. This chapter makes a distinction between attitudes and spiritual dispositions. Do you agree? Why?

CHAPTER FIVE

Pillar One: Teacher Knowledge

What Do Christian Educators Need to Know?

Teacher knowledge is the first pillar of Christian education. It encompasses five areas of information every teacher should have: knowledge of God, the Bible, learners, available resources, and the power of Christian education. Not every person who enters Christian education training has mastered all five areas. Even veteran teachers may not be completely comfortable in each. This chapter identifies content for initial teacher training and serves as a guide to topics that can be further explored in continuing training sessions.

Teachers Need to Know God

"Theology" literally means to study God. Stone and Duke in their book, *How to Think Theologically*, describe theology as the "process of thinking about life in light of the faith that Christians engage in because of their calling."[64] Studying God is not a task reserved for those in seminaries and Bible colleges. It is the responsibility of all Christians. By virtue of their faith, believers are compelled to know God. Baptism into the death, burial, and resurrection of Jesus Christ urges Christians to explore the nature of this Divine Being who is

God in the Bible, the world, and human lives. Christian educators cannot shy away from the theological task of knowing more about this Holy God for whom they have declared their love. A confession of faith necessitates that believers do the work of theology.

Knowing God is a pre-condition for teaching in the church. In Psalm 119:2, the psalmist admonishes us to take the responsibility to "seek Him with the whole heart." Jesus said, "Take my yoke upon you, and learn of me..." (Matthew 11:29). When Jesus spoke with Nicodemus, He said, "You must be born again" (John 3:7). These mandates apply to everyone in the faith community. Before taking a Christian education assignment, teachers must be able to share their faith stories as indicators that they are not seekers struggling to gain a spiritual identity. A teacher's knowledge of God through rebirth kindles the urgency of teaching for transformation.

The five features of learning listed in chapter four also represent the knowledge teachers must have. Teachers' attitudes, behaviors, and spiritual dispositions are windows into their knowledge of and relationship with God. Teachers' attitudes toward learners and the teaching ministry reveal whether they believe that spiritual transformation is possible. When teachers know God, it is revealed in their behavior. It is seen in their interaction with class members and people in their faith community (Hebrews 10:25). The spiritual dispositions of teachers demonstrate their confidence that the Holy Spirit is operational in their lives. Teachers who do not value and nurture their spiritual dispositions fail to grasp the transformative power of the teaching ministry. Whether teachers understand that biblical content has an eternal purpose will be revealed through spiritual disposition. If teachers are unsure of the importance of God in their lives, they will not convince learners that knowing God is essential for their lives.

Teachers Need to Know the Bible

Psalm 119:11 summarizes why knowing the Bible is important: "Thy word have I hid in mine heart that I might not sin against thee." In order to hide God's Word in their hearts, teachers need to know more than the names of the sixty-six books in order. At the very least, those who seek to participate in the teaching ministry should be Bible readers.

As a baseline, teachers should complete a class that provides an overview of the Bible so they can understand the connection between the Old and New Testaments and be familiar with the people and events in the Bible. This brief exposure will not provide everything teachers need to understand about the theological concepts they will encounter in planning and delivering Bible lessons. It will, however, prepare them for more in-depth knowledge. Through ongoing preparation, teachers will come to know historical contexts, literary types, language, doctrines, and other Bible essentials.

Studying the Bible is not a perfunctory task. It is not tangential to teaching; it is the basis of the work of Christian education. Teachers cannot view the Bible as a series of stories that people should know. It is more than just one book in their personal collections. Congregational teachers should place value on the role of the Bible in the transformation process. Studying the Bible is a spiritual endeavor, powerful enough to call teachers to renewed understandings of its tenets and their faith. With the help of the Holy Spirit and a systematic approach to teacher development, every teacher can come to recognize the depth of the relationship between the Bible and his or her ministry to the congregation.

Teachers Need to Know the Learners

All teachers must know the general characteristics of the learners before them. Because knowing learners means knowing more than assumptions and profiles, teachers must strive to personally know the people in their classes. To some congregational teachers, knowing each person's name seems sufficient. (It is not, and shame on all those teachers who don't know their students' names and don't mind that the students don't know theirs!) This doesn't mean that a teacher must strike up a friendship with every student in the class, but teachers should be at least familiar with learners' interests, families, cultures, and spiritual needs. This does not give teachers a license to pry; it does give them a reason to pay attention.

Knowing students enables teachers to appreciate learners' struggles with applying the Bible to their lives. Class discussion is one window that can reveal learners' hearts, but there are others. Questionnaires such as those found in Appendix A can provide a starting point. Those who teach children and youth may decide to make home visits or have class outings. Adult teachers may find it enjoyable to have coffee with groups of class members. Sending notes during family crises or cards for birthdays and anniversaries provides opportunities to touch students' lives.

Knowing students also means that teachers recognize learners' religious backgrounds. Teachers should not assume that every person seated before them has been involved in congregational life since childhood. Congregants who have not been previously exposed to church life or who came from another faith tradition may not be familiar with the order of service or statements of faith. Nor should teachers assume that those who have religious upbringing have committed their lives to Christ. Being in church does not mean that a person is committed to the faith or even knows what that commitment entails. These are concerns that can be surfaced only as teachers interact with students and pay attention to the issues and questions they have.

Technology has become an essential part of the communication between teachers and students. While new social media options are available every day, platforms like Facebook and Instagram as well as texts and e-mails connect classes between sessions. Using these tools can help teachers stay abreast of students' needs or discuss questions about lessons. Telephone prayer lines are still a strong method of support for some individuals and groups. Time spent calling, texting, or emailing class members to see how the week is going is time well spent. Teachers have a responsibility, however, to be sure that protocols are in place that protect student confidentiality as well as guarding against any predatory or illegal actions on anyone's part. Although technology keeps us connected, the abuse of these media is always a concern. Teachers should speak with ministry leaders to apprise them of how they are using technology and to make sure that no church policies or legal issues are breached.

Going Beyond the Classroom

To know learners more personally, congregational teachers may want to take advantage of opportunities to gather with participants outside of class. Special outings such as plays or sporting events can provide a change of scenery. (The expectation of fun can also change relationships.) Service and missions projects build community and foster connections as class members act on their faith. These might include community clean-ups executed as part of a whole-church effort. Some projects can be implemented with partner organizations. Examples might include preparing meals for parents whose children are in the hospital or gathering personal hygiene items for families in local shelters. Whether organized by individual teachers or ministry leaders, class outings, service projects, and mission activities help learners and teachers develop confidence in the gifts and skills they contribute to the faith community.

Christian educators who facilitate projects like these are often surprised at the knowledge and abilities of participants. This was the reaction of teachers when several churches partnered with a community organization to complete a mission project with junior students. The event was part of a weeklong, day-camp program. In the culminating activity, the children were to help feed homeless members of the community. During the daily camp activities, two boys were unruly in every session. It became so bad that the teachers requested to ban the two boys from the final activity. Permission was denied. On the day of the culminating activity, the boys proved to be the hardest workers and the most eager volunteers. They helped to move food crates in preparation for lunch. They were courteous to the people who came to eat and helpful to children and seniors who needed assistance. They were the first to help clean the area after the meal. In debriefing, teachers found that in their local churches these two children had developed the skill to help. They wanted to be counted as meaningful contributors to a worthwhile event. That event gave them the opportunity to do so and helped teachers understand the value of such outside ventures.

Staying Connected to the Real World

Teachers should be connected to the world around them because it is the world that shapes learners' lives. They need not engage in activities that are harmful physically, emotionally, or spiritually just to experience what students are doing. Teachers cannot refuse to acknowledge pop culture, read books and newspapers, or listen to music that does not extol the Gospel. If they do, they will soon be out of touch with those they teach.

One gen-xer confessed that he grew up enjoying hip-hop, rap, and house music. Consequently, his car speakers were accustomed to those sounds until the day he heard himself singing along. At that point, he realized that he was cursing and speaking disparagingly about women, practices he actually abhorred. Even though he was reading his Bible, praying daily, and seeking to be uplifted spiritually, his music was part of his psyche. He knew he had been Spirit-filled, but his actions and tastes did not reflect his relationship with God.

In that moment, he understood that his attitude and spiritual disposition had changed. He was no longer comfortable with his music choices. While he liked some of the same traditional hymns and gospel music artists as his parents, he felt too young to make that the only thing on his playlist. Still, he realized the need to feed his spirit with "psalms and hymns and spiritual songs, singing and making melody in your heart to the Lord" (Ephesians 5:19). His solution was simple: he switched to gospel hip-hop. While some may frown at his solution, teachers must realize that spiritual development comes in many guises. Teachers must be prepared to know learners well enough to support them in their efforts to develop spiritual strength through practices of faith—even if those avenues are very different from their own.

Maintaining a Spiritual Connection

Prayer cannot be overlooked as a tool for knowing students. Prayer keeps learners' hearts on teachers' minds. When teachers pray for their students, opportunities to know participants better will become available. When class members share prayer requests or other concerns, they are revealing their personal lives and interests. This gives teachers sincere reasons to pray for those they teach. No matter the size or location of the congregation, teachers should always pray for students. Regardless of which age group congregational teachers serve, they must have compassion and concern for the learners before them. No one can teach scriptural content and encourage spiritual transformation without touching lives with spiritual actions. When teachers know students and are Spirit-led in their concerns, they pray for learners knowing that their prayers and actions can make a difference. That difference can be transformative.

Teachers Need to Know the Available Resources

Resources include materials and technologies that help get the job done. The adage to "work smarter not harder" is made possible through the incorporation of physical and electronic resources. Teachers don't have to "re-invent the wheel." Some would say (with tongue in cheek) that if "every good and perfect gift comes from above" (James 1:17), then perhaps God is pleased when teachers use available resources to enhance how students learn about their faith. The key is knowing what is available and how to use it as a support rather than the focus of Christian teaching.

Resources for congregational teaching can include everything from curricular materials and transportation for mission trips, to space in the church building and furnishings in the classroom. In teaching children, resources may range from crayons to choir bells. The scope of curricular materials in one church might be restricted to pencils, projectors, and a photocopier. Another church may have sophisticated, high-resolution resources of all types. Some churches require learners to bring Bibles; others have Bibles available for in-class use. No matter the situation, teachers must know what is available, the policies and practices that govern their use, and how to take advantage of the resources in their instructional program.

One area that too often doesn't get mentioned until it is too late is money. In many churches, students (especially adults) must purchase their own books. In other churches, a budget may be available for items ranging from snacks to workbooks. No matter the congregation size, Christian education programs operate on a limited budget based on the overall church budget. Teachers must be aware of the limitations regarding what can be spent and by whom. They should be told in advance (and should ask) about reimbursement of monies spent on class projects or activities. If church policy allows teachers to spend money, teachers should know what is appropriate and what is allowed; policies on what can be purchased or brought in for sharing should be clear.

Print Materials

The most common printed resources are books and supplemental materials. These can range from books by well-known authors or Sunday school curricula, to books assigned for special classes and materials used to enhance teachers' personal study. Professionally published curricular materials are usually well-written and researched. They generally identify teaching aims, Bible background, and church history. Most published curricula provide strategies for opening the class, examining the biblical text, and extending the learning experience beyond the initial class encounter. Publishers work hard to produce materials that are age-appropriate and address the experiences congregants may be facing. However, if teachers are unaware of these features, they may misuse the materials or forego the benefits they provide.

Design is another major factor in Christian education resources. This aspect of the material selection often gets swept aside. It shouldn't. Print and electronic media, advertising, and personal computers have created a generation of consumers who respond (consciously or subconsciously) to the use of color, graphics, and layout. Locally produced or copied resources that lack appeal in style, color, or content send a message that the teaching is less than stellar as well.

Independent publishers produce materials for a wide range of cultures and faith traditions. Churches and Christian education departments should make sure that the resources are appropriate for their congregation and align with the theological and doctrinal standards of the faith tradition. Anything detected to be a problem or controversy should be explored and discussed by teachers and leaders before class. Doctrinal and ecclesial matters such as modes of baptism or communion practices may need to be addressed to insure that teachers are comfortable and knowledgeable about what they are sharing with students. Teachers and Christian education leaders should be familiar with their resources and raise concerns where needed.

Congregational teachers should know how and when to supplement their own knowledge with additional study. While many print resources are available to teachers, it is not necessary that instructors own, or even consult, every commentary and lexicon. Many of the traditional materials used in Bible study are available online or electronically. They are often less expensive, more varied, and more accessible than hard-copy versions. Still, their use requires teachers to know how to critically select reliable references. Using the Internet to consult a "wiki" is not likely to give the most scholarly and accurate information. Teachers who understand these supplemental resources and how to use them will dig more deeply to comprehend Bible passages and extend their knowledge as part of their ongoing learning.

Technology

Technology has changed how people learn as they encounter the world around them. The United States Department of Education's 2010 National Education Technology Plan called for recognizing "that technology is at the core of virtually every aspect of our daily lives and work, and we must leverage it to provide engaging and powerful learning experiences and content."[65] Using technology for instructional purposes is no longer a trend. It is a way of learning, a path to educational outcomes.

Churches once relied on radio and public access cable television to help spread the Gospel. Today, churches include websites, YouTube channels, Facebook Live, and other social media in their ministry outreach. Finances, the size of the congregation, and church theology may also determine if technology is available for in-class use. Some churches have incorporated technology directly into the teaching-learning environment. SMART boards, projection devices, and digital technologies have made congregational classrooms (and some sanctuaries) more interactive and interesting.[66]

The generation born after 1998 is called "digital natives." These are the "'native speakers' of the digital language of computers, video games and the Internet."[67] A study by the Pew Foundation found that 39% of students in secular education sites use smartphones to do their homework. Thirty-one percent use tablets for that purpose. Since many schools are lagging behind in supplying technology, some school districts have enacted a Bring-Your-Own-Device (BYOD) policy.

If secular education sees the need to be creative in incorporating technology, Christian education cannot be left behind. Churches must recognize how students learn and tap into those ideas that work. In local congregations, people bring their cell phones and tablets to look up Bible passages and take notes on sermons. Tweeting has replaced the "amen corner" in some churches. Individuals use FaceBook Live to share lessons and sermons with friends in real time. Teachers should be knowledgeable about the technologies people use and consider ways to incorporate some of these into the learning experience.

While technology has added a new dimension, Christian educators do not need to include every bell and whistle in order to have an effective program. In fact, technology overkill can destroy a lesson. Balance is important because Christian education has arrived at a technological crossroad. It is time to embrace the wise use of technological resources and appreciate their role in the Christian learning community.

Teachers Need to Know the Power of Christian Education

Teaching in churches today means knowing how to use curriculum design and instructional tools to engage learners and foster spiritual transformation. The children, youth, and young adults who participate in Christian education today are products of new ways of teaching and learning. They have been using cooperative learning groups and technology for most, or all, of their lives. They have a right to expect that the strategies for learning in their Christian experiences should be compatible with their secular classrooms. Even adults who have not been to school in years are not content to sit through lectures. Christian education today cannot escape its connection to the world of learning and curriculum design. Today's classrooms are flexible and active. Christian educators must be creative in their efforts to address the human yearning for God.

Christian education, however, occurs in sacred spaces and for divine purposes. For that reason, congregational teaching has a dimension that is lacking in the secular setting. When congregational teachers recognize the role of the Holy Spirit in their work, their perspective of the power of congregational teaching is heightened. Congregational teaching is not a perfunctory act; it should never be approached without prayer and the acknowledgment that it is a spiritual undertaking. The power of Christian education lies in the craft of teaching, the environment surrounding it, and the expectation of the Spirit's guidance.

The Power of Craft

Training programs must help teachers employ the science and art of teaching. Teachers must adopt the artistic elements of imagination, instinct, performance, and style because these are characteristics that create phenomena. Unlike purely physical or social experiences, phenomena are experiences that are unusual enough to leave a lasting impression because they carry emotional and psychological meaning. The assassinations of John F. Kennedy and Martin Luther King, Jr. are still vividly recalled by a generation who experienced them. The tragedies of Hurricane Katrina, Sandy Hook, and Stoneman Douglas High School in Parkland, Florida, permanently changed the lives of those involved and the people who experienced them through real-time media accounts. These events moved from short-term memory to long-term memory in such a dramatic way that people recall where they were when the stories broke on the news. Every meaningful phenomenon is not a tragedy. (Consider the birth of a child, for example.) However, all meaningful phenomena are mentally processed and rehearsed because they significantly change perceptions.

Because of its ability to meld emotional, psychological, and spiritual aspects of the encounters, congregational teaching can create phenomenological impressions on learners. Imagine two instructors who teach the same lesson using the same plan or outline. Each is able to execute the skill called teaching adequately, but are the classes the same? One teacher covers the material but creates a boring experience. The other achieves the identified goals but artfully guides learners to reconsider their assumptions as they make decisions and judgments based on the encounter. In this way, the second teacher creates a phenomenal experience that has the potential to be remembered, cherished, and applied. These are the results that congregational teaching seeks to achieve.

Given such potential, every aspect of the teaching encounter is important. The events in any teaching-learning experience are perceived differently by each person involved. Each learner's personal circumstance and prior knowledge will contribute to the impression left by the events of the class encounter. No two people experience a teaching-learning episode in exactly the same way. Where one person may immediately understand a concept and make life-connections, another may consider the information impractical. (Remember that subject you hated in school because it would never be useful in real life?)

The science of education draws on the basic educational tools of teaching, learning, and curricular intent. These tools help churches create educational programs that address teaching, discipleship, leadership development, and spiritual transformation. Research on teaching and learning helps Christian educators understand how lessons can be developed and what resources work best. Current research on memory and the brain can help teachers understand how students process and apply lesson information. Books, podcasts, and online resources on these subjects are plentiful and easily accessed. As Christian educators realize that the resources of the larger educational arena are at their disposal, they have the freedom to adopt and adapt these tools.

Because we are "fearfully and wonderfully made," each of us has unique learning styles that help us gain and process information (Psalm 139:14). Because all learners are different, a teacher's creativity can provide several encounters with lesson concepts. Sharing a photograph of the Holy Land or a model of the Ark can spark learners' imaginations and make a point clear. Tracing Paul's steps on a map or making a replica of Moses' rod appeals to those learners who learn best by tactile or physical means. Singing a hymn or reciting the lyrics to a gospel chorus can drive a lesson concept home. Teachers must prayerfully rely on their instincts and creativity to incorporate the art and science of teaching into each lesson.

The Power of Environment

Christian teaching anticipates the sacred nature of its undertaking. This does not mean that children won't be messy and loud. It does not mean that youth must pretend to be "saintly" or that adults are restricted from being honest about their lives. Christian teaching is sacred because of the spiritual nature of the encounter: the interaction with the Word of God and the development of faith. This does not mean that everything that occurs in the congregational classroom is directly sanctioned by the divine presence! The classroom or any setting for instruction involves people and ideas that can enhance, change or even disrupt the encounter. In order for teachers to effectively handle all of the factors at work in any class, they must also be aware of influences that can alter the learning environment and hinder the psychological, emotional, and spiritual dynamic of the instruction.

Environment includes the arrangement of furniture in the room, as well as clutter and noise. These things may seem small, but the environment of the teaching space can hinder or help students to see, hear, or remember what is going on in the room. The interplay between learners is also an environmental issue. Lively discussions, interactive exercises, even periods of reflection and silence can help students with varied learning styles. On the other hand, side conversations distract learners and become disruptive. Not addressing the student who "hogs" the conversation can destroy class morale. Teachers of children need to balance the lesson so that students who are able to read, or who are more advanced in some areas, don't dominate the class and leave less knowledgeable learners to be embarrassed or hurt. Insensitivity by teachers or students to cultural or social factors can leave learners of any age feeling left out or disrespected. How teachers address environmental issues can be important to achieving the outcomes of any lesson.

Every aspect of the class encounter teaches. Every lesson is planned to convey a specific idea in order to achieve a specific outcome. These are the obvious or explicit curricular choices that govern the lesson. But there are "hidden curricula" that interfere with learning and change the environment of the encounter.[68] For example, selecting only the male students for special projects tells the females in class that their voices don't count. When Mother's Day cards are created without considering that some children's mothers might be deceased or other children may be in foster care, it can make those children think that their situations and pain are unimportant. When the entire kindergarten Sunday school class is on the Easter program, the child who does not have a new outfit learns that he or she doesn't fit. Teachers may unconsciously favor the responses of prominent church members leaving the adult newcomers to wonder if their presence is welcomed. Awareness of the hidden curricula challenges Christian educators to pay attention to every aspect of the learning environment and the lesson. When Christian educators are aware of the class environment, they are better equipped to address the spiritual needs of all learners.

The Power of the Divine

While the craft of teaching and knowledge of the impediments to teaching are important, they are not enough to galvanize the power of congregational teaching. As the Holy Spirit is active in these processes, the power of the Divine is at work in the hearts of individual learners. The presence of God is the ingredient that forges lasting change. The content of teaching is the Bible, the record of God in action with humanity. It is Bible-centered teaching coupled with the presence of the Holy Spirit that activates the power of Christian education. Psalm 1:1–3 provides a frame for understanding this:

> *Blessed is the man that walketh not in the counsel of the ungodly, nor standeth in the way of sinners, nor sitteth in the seat of the scornful. But his delight is in the law of the LORD; and in his law doth he meditate day and night. And he shall be like a tree planted by the rivers of water, that bringeth forth his fruit in his season; his leaf also shall not wither; and whatsoever he doeth shall prosper.*

- *Christian education is powerful because it is anchored in the Bible.* The *Jewish Study Bible* explains that the uniqueness of Psalm 1 lies in its emphasis on the virtues of reading God's Word rather than human observations based on study of God's Word.[69] Through the precepts of God's law, Christian education calls believers to expect the promises of God, to know the character of God, and to honor the presence of God in their lives.

- *Christian education is powerful because it presents an image of the Christian life.* This image results from adherence to the Word of God. Those who embrace God's Word are blessed as a result of their study. Blessedness is not predicated on position or fortune. It is not a state of perpetual bliss. False promises of endless prosperity and acquisition of authority do not square with this view of the Christian life. Christian education keeps the image of Christian life in focus as it encourages participants to examine their lives against the backdrop of God's promises and earth's daily realities.

- *Christian education is powerful because it provides direction for living.* It is in God that "we live and move and have our being" (Acts 17:28) Life is not stagnant. At various times in life we walk, stand, or sit. Everyone experiences the journey at different paces and through different trials. At each juncture, however, we must ascertain where we are. When students experience pain or disappointment, Christian education challenges them not to accept scornful dispositions that reject God and seek unfruitful alternative pathways. Congregational teaching provides a window through which students can determine if they are following God's path or the path of those who scorn God. Christian education develops community and reveals the testimonial footsteps of those who have gone before and weathered the storm.

- *Christian education is powerful because it provides the space and freedom to practice faith.* Psalms is the book of prayers. Through Christian education, individuals learn to pray and join collectively in prayer for others in the faith community. In the practices of faith, we find delight. This is not because we do not experience struggle. It is because meditating on the Word of God provides the freedom to question our circumstance. Meditation and prayer provide the space needed to fully embrace God's promises. Christian education helps students develop faith that is anchored in the confidence of hope and the assurance of deliverance (Hebrews 11:1). Christian education ensures students that through their tears they need not be afraid to say, "Lord, I believe; help thou mine unbelief" (Mark 9:24).

- *Christian education is powerful because it nurtures students of all ages.* Regardless of age, students are encouraged to thrive in their faith. Christian education provides what learners need to be fruitful and share their faith with others. It emboldens them to continue trusting God despite the storms. It supports learners as they grow in the grace of God. Christian education instills confidence that in each season of life, those who embrace the Word of God will flourish.

Summary

Teacher knowledge as a pillar of Christian education prepares congregational teachers to effectively practice the art and science of teaching. This involves the efforts of Christian educators to know their students and their students' learning styles. The art of teaching engages creativity and gives attention to the environment of each encounter. Congregational teachers must be good stewards of the resources that assist them in achieving teaching aims and learning targets. Teacher knowledge of God and the Bible recognizes the power of the Holy Spirit to infuse the lesson, guide the teacher, and enrich the students.

Consider:

1. Reflect on your faith journey and identify how you came to know God.
2. This chapter proposes that teachers must do more than just say they know God. Do you believe that knowing God and being in relationship with God are prerequisites for teaching? Create criteria for determining how teacher knowledge determines if individuals should become teachers.
3. This chapter identifies five areas of teacher knowledge. List the five areas and identify at least one additional reason that teachers should know each.
4. In your opinion, what level of Bible knowledge should be required for those who are entering the teaching ministry?
5. This chapter identified several ways for teachers to become more familiar with their students. Is getting to know learners really important? Why? What additional strategies can you offer to help this process?
6. Make a list of the resources your church has available for use by teachers. What rules and guidelines govern the use of these resources?
7. List the elements you think can positively or negatively affect the teaching environment. Explain.
8. What do you see as the power of Christian education? Why?

CHAPTER SIX

Pillar Two: Bible-Centered Teaching

Encountering the Bible: The Ultimate Phenomenon

Jesus' Crucifixion is recorded in Mark 15:25–41. It is one event, one phenomenon, that elicited a different response from each person present. As you read the text, you can almost hear the religious leaders and members of the crowd as they hurl insults. You can visualize the women who were grieved, speechless, and helpless. You somehow focus on the soldier guarding the Cross and note how captivated he was by the sight of Jesus. You can imagine how humbled he became with the revelation that this man was the Son of God. From the sounds and sights of Mark's account, fast forward to recall your first encounter with this text. Try to recall your realization of Jesus' substitutionary death on your behalf. Think about how you have re-experienced this singular event with each reading, each sermon, each lesson, and each creative re-enactment of that day. Finally, consider how others who follow Jesus today feel when they internalize His sacrifice at Calvary. While Jesus' Crucifixion occurred over two thousand years ago, it is understood differently, but just as powerfully, by each person who finds himself or herself at the foot of the Cross.

Spiritual history and transformative hope are compacted into the moment of Jesus' Crucifixion. The power of Jesus' sacrifice on the Cross remains an efficacious truth, fully active in human lives from that moment until this. For thousands of years, the phenomenal events recorded in the Bible have been re-experienced by Christian communities. When Bible students prayerfully seek to understand and apply biblical principles, they too re-enter those moments and are positioned for spiritual transformation.

The Power of the Biblical Text

Information and transformation are the objectives of biblical interpretation and at the center of Christian education.[70] The information is drawn from the historic nature of the text and its meaning for the original audience. Yet the Bible is not content to give us information. Instead, it leads us to transformation, a "complete change in character or condition."[71] This change in life-direction results, in part, from our effort to glean meaning from our encounters with God through the Bible. The Bible is about God. It records His love for humanity and tells His salvific desire toward a fallen people. It explains God's redemptive plan and His desire for the redeemed to share eternity. In essence, the Bible records the transforming account of a transcendent God who is "exalted above the created universe, so far above that it reaches beyond time and space—forward and backward—to the point that human thought cannot imagine it."[72]

The power of the Bible lies in its revelation and inspiration. "It is God Himself who puts in our hearts to seek Him and makes it possible in the same measure to know Him."[73] The revelation of God is seen in "the creation, history, the conscience of man…"[74] It is through the Bible's inspirational nature and authority that God has uniquely revealed Himself to humankind (Romans 16:25; 2 Timothy 3:16–17). Therefore, the Old Testament is more than the history of the Jewish people. It foretells Christ's coming and points to the extent of God's love toward humanity (Isaiah 9:6). The New Testament is more than the record of Jesus on earth. It confirms the Old Testament and forecasts Jesus' return amidst the revelation of God in flesh. Because the Bible's power is seen in its revelation of the eternal God in our mortal situations, Bible-centered teaching helps congregants reflect on the ways their encounters with the self-existent and all powerful God transform their lives.[75]

The Purpose of Bible-Centered Teaching

Bible-centered teaching should help congregants think about the Bible, not to produce an analysis that destroys faith but to approach the biblical text as "faith seeking understanding."[76] The ministry of teaching aims for transformation and application as it equips learners to be independent students of God's Word. Bible-centered teaching provides learners with the tools of interpretation that uncover the meaning of biblical texts and foster spiritual maturity. Bible-centered teaching aims to help students develop positive attitudes and strengthen spiritual dispositions as they seek the Holy Spirit for understanding and direction. Learners then increasingly approach Bible study with hearts that are humble, teachable, and willing to glean new insight and guidance.[77] Thus, when learners gain confidence in seeking God on their own, they are prepared for a lifetime of transformative faith that infuses every area of their lives.

The Bible is at the core of the congregational teaching endeavor. That does not mean every class must be solely about the Bible. For example, if a church joins forces with a financial institution to provide classes on home purchases and money management, the course will involve members of the congregation. Even if Christian education members only facilitate the sessions, they should do so in the context of Christian living. While the financial institution will teach the class, the congregational setting requires the incorporation of biblical principles. This might include opening class with Scripture reading and prayer. The Christian education department might supplement the institution's materials by distributing a list of Scriptures related to the topic. The key is that the financial principles are aligned with biblical principles. Christianity is not a garment that is appropriate in one setting but not the other. Being people of faith means "viewing our lives in light of the Gospel."[78] A Bible-based ideology of teaching sees to it that all congregational instruction gives preference to the biblical principles that govern Christian living.

Roadblocks to Bible-Centered Learning

Bible-centered lessons begin with reading the Bible; however, there are at least three reasons that it is sometimes difficult for learners to begin with the biblical text. First, given the plethora of commentaries and devotionals available, many people do not recognize the need to begin with the Scriptural record. While these resources are wonderful helps to understanding and applying the Word of God, starting with a commentary assures that study begins with the assumptions and ideas of the commentator. It is difficult to discern what a passage might be saying to your specific situation if you have started from someone else's point of view. Beginning with a devotional or commentary insures that the reader will examine the text in light of that central thought. When learners begin their study or daily devotion by at least reading the actual biblical text, they allow the words of the text to initially resonate in their hearts.

The second roadblock to starting with the Bible is the learner's ability to comprehend the words of the text. Learners need Bibles they can understand. While some people frown on any version other than the one their church sanctions, the Bibles we have today are actually copies made over centuries of earlier documents written in different languages. Embedded in biblical documents is information representative of various cultures over time. While "all scripture is given by inspiration of God, and is profitable for doctrine, for reproof, for correction, for instruction in righteousness" (2 Timothy 3:16), no current Bible has the exact wording of the original texts. Translations, therefore, are necessary to make the Scriptures clear to a modern audience.

Teachers should familiarize their students with assorted and reliable translations. When learners have Bibles they understand, they begin the process of study and meditation as more confident and independent students of God's Word. At the very least, readers should be aware that comparing the language in several translations can help clarify meanings.

Finally, a reader's approach to the Bible can make understanding difficult. There are people who view the Bible literally—word for word—and give little thought to its cohesive structure. The Bible text is true, but taking the words out of context can cause confusion. Theologian Thomas Long warns that biblical texts must not be "seen as jars with eternal meaning inside but as interactive fields of meaning."[79] To aid in identifying "interactive fields of meaning," there are two ways to approach Bible study: exegesis and eisegesis. Exegesis is the act of drawing meaning from biblical texts for the purpose of the practical application of Scripture. Eisegesis, on the other hand, is reading meaning into the text by assigning a predetermined meaning to the Scriptures. When the Bible is approached in a way that puts meaning into the Scriptures rather than seeking what the Scriptures are saying to the reader, students miss the original meaning as well as the literary richness of the message the text seeks to convey. Likewise, when students approach the biblical text by relying on what they have heard or believed to be true about it, they limit their ability to gain inspiration and understanding that is applicable to their personal situations.

The Process of Bible-Centered Teaching

A major criticism of congregational teaching has been that it lacks scholarship and reflection. Critics see congregational teaching, particularly through the lens of Sunday school, as a random reading of Bible "stories." In order to elevate the perception and role of congregational teaching, Christian educators must question how they engage learners in Bible study. Reading the Bible is always a positive behavior, but what benefit is to be gained from selecting a few isolated verses to read with your morning coffee? Randomly selecting verses divorces them from their context and does not help in understanding the whole of either the passage or the book under study.

Studying the Bible requires more than just reading a published version of its text. A. W. Tozer points out that

> The Bible is the written word of God, and because it is written it is confined and limited by the necessities of ink and paper . . . The voice of God, however, is alive and free as the sovereign is free.... God's word in the Bible can have power only because it corresponds to God's word in the universe. It is the present Voice which makes the written word all-powerful.[80]

Studying the Bible, therefore, means engaging the Logos, the Word, which became flesh (John 1:14). Doing this requires a methodical approach that "enables us to teach ourselves and others what the whole Bible (Old and New Testaments) says, thus fulfilling . . . the Great Commission."[81] It involves using the proper tools to unearth meaning and apply biblical truths to daily experiences. A theological approach to Bible study helps believers make better decisions about daily encounters in order to become better Christians.[82]

A Bible-centered approach to congregational teaching and learning equips teachers to fulfill their responsibility to share Bible study methods with learners. When learners are taught to exegete Bible texts, they learn that there are no "secrets" to studying the Bible independently. Learners need strategies for reading the Bible that help them think about what it says and how that applies to their lives.

Bible Study Methods

Determining which Bible study methods are most helpful is an important skill. Teachers can encourage this by modeling a variety of methods in their teaching. The decision regarding which methods will depend on the class, the purpose, and the text under study. Mastering various methodologies takes time and more instruction than this book can offer. Teachers should take advantage of resources that can help them learn and share strategies that are appropriate for their group.

Basic Strategies

Basic strategies are aimed at introducing individuals and groups to examining Scriptures. These methods can be used in class to teach adults, youth, and children. Modifications may be needed to help some persons begin these processes. For example, the most basic modification of the inductive study method uses three basic questions: What does the passage say? What does it mean? What is it saying to me for my life? Basic Bible study strategies include (but are not limited to) the following:

- **Inductive Bible Study** – Engages a pattern of observation, interpretation, and application to understand the relationship between verses in a given passage and encourage reflective application.
- **Survey Study** – Seeks to determine how a specific book or Testament is organized by examining background, author, outline of events, etc.
- **Topical Study** – Examines the themes presented across various books of the Bible.
- **Biographical Study** – Considers specific biblical figures by identifying who they were as well as their backgrounds, significance, and relationship to other figures.
- **Word Study** – Focuses on understanding concepts by exploring the words that express them. This requires specialized resources such as concordances and lexicons to examine words in their original language and then discover the nuances presented in English.
- **Devotional Study** – Organizes daily inspirational reading for systematic reflection and application.

Critical Approaches

Criticism is the act of observing, interpreting, and analyzing Scripture in order to better understand and apply it. "Biblical criticism (is the) discipline that studies textual, compositional, and historical questions surrounding the Old and New Testaments.[83] Critical approaches to biblical exegesis provide a starting point for digging more deeply into biblical texts. These forms of critical analysis have a rich history in theological study and specific protocols. Those who use them should first spend time studying their purposes, principles, and guidelines. Because critical approaches developed over time, often one concept may encompass or be the basis of another. There can be significant overlap. The list below identifies only a few approaches; yet, some may represent only one aspect of a larger approach. A few of the more common critical approaches are

- **Form Criticism** – Begins with an understanding of the oral tradition of biblical texts as the basis for analyzing the technical properties of the Bible book or of the Old or New Testament by examining language, genre, structure, tone, arrangement, etc.[84]
- **Historical Criticism** – Examines the biblical text in order to determine the history "of the text" (why and when it was written, etc.) as well as the history "in the text" (the historical, political, religious, social context it records).[85]
- **Textural Criticism** – Provides insight into meanings and original language as often seen in various translations of the text that attempt to explain the original language of a passage.
- **Literary Criticism** – Concerns "a family of diverse approaches" to exegesis.[86] For example, Old Testament Literary criticism is concerned with the sources of the oral texts as well as authorship, setting, and other aspects of the current format of the text.
- **Narrative Criticism** – Examines what Mark Allen Powell calls "Scripture as Story," which allows one to examine such aspects of the text as point of view, plot, symbolism, etc.[87]

Helps for Biblical Familiarity and Literacy

The study methods above provide a range of strategies for vigorous study of the Bible. Nevertheless, there is a need to provide beginning learners with tools that increase their familiarity with the Bible and their comfort in using it. Christian educators must be willing to help learners gain basic literacy skills. It should not be assumed that everyone—including adults—is biblically literate or even familiar with the Bible. Some Christian education departments offer age-appropriate classes that familiarize new converts with this information. Even if no specific classes are offered, congregational teachers should be mindful of when learners need clarification to understand specific terms, concepts, rituals, or sacraments.

The most basic understanding of the Bible begins with knowing how it is organized, how to find the various books, and how to identify Scripture references. For new Christians, these skills are critical because they go to the heart of physically using the Bible as a resource and being able to communicate where passages and concepts are located.

The role of memorization cannot be overlooked in helping develop biblical familiarity and literacy. For example, most Christians know Matthew 6:9–13 (The Lord's Prayer), John 3:16, and Psalm 23; however, there are other Scriptures that are either commonly memorized or that serve as personal affirmation and encouragement. When learners are encouraged to memorize Scripture, they internalize the message the passage presents.

Class and individual activities such as games, puzzles, and drills help learners acquire literacy skills and reinforce familiarity with Bible books, people, events, and passages. While these are often used with children, they should not be limited to the young. Adults, too, enjoy Bible puzzles and games. Teaching resources are available that provide suggestions for using such helps in classes at all levels.

A Panoramic View of Biblical Texts: PERSIA

The Bible study processes shared with congregational students generally refer to internal investigations of the biblical text. It is also important that Bible-centered teaching provide a "big picture" that helps participants relate the encounters in the Bible text to the general landscape of history. The adaptation of an historical investigative tool known as PERSIA can help learners and teachers gain a broad perspective of the biblical text. The point of this study is to investigate the religious, cultural, language, and population patterns of Bible passages. This process has proven to be useful in introducing congregational teachers and students to a procedure for examining the physical and cultural geography of the Bible.[88]

The process is straightforward and simple. It uses a series of questions in connection with the acronym PERSIA. Each letter identifies a key historic component present in any epoch. When geographical and archaeological findings of that period are added to the study, learners are able to better visualize and connect the human and divine aspects of the biblical record.

The questions listed represent starting points for the exploration of each section of the PERSIA model. They can be used to guide student observations of the text, lead class discussions, or introduce the need for further research. While the six areas are discernible in every epoch, not all questions are appropriate to every passage under study. Teachers and learners should add or modify questions based on their observations and study.

P – Politics – Searching for the political interactions in the biblical text leads to the study of governments including their infrastructures, functions, influences, and authority. Questions in this category seek to determine the forms of government as well as the political groups and individuals who represent the centers of power. It also looks for people and people groups who are marginalized by the political structure.

- What form of government is described in the lesson (monarchy, theocracy, etc.)

- What political ruler is mentioned or prevalent in the text? How did this person gain power?
- What other government officials are mentioned and how are they related?
- Is there a political structure to any religious parties or other groups mentioned in the text?
- What legal processes and interactions are mentioned in the text?
- How many nations are discussed in the text? What is their relationship?

E – Economics – This area investigates the access, distribution, consumption, and production of wealth and resources. This set of questions seeks to identify the economic formats and systems that are present in the passage under study.

- Does the lesson discuss currency, barter, or trade?
- What form of currency or wealth is used and how much is it worth in US dollars or other world currencies today? (For example, how much is a shekel worth today?)
- What measurements are used and how do they relate to US or metric measurements? (For example, how big is a cubit?)
- What forms of economy or economic worth (crops, animals, minerals, etc.) are mentioned in the text?
- Did the Scripture passage refer to people who were employed by others? What status is assigned to each party?
- Does the text involve slaves, indentured servants, or other persons who are deemed to be property? Are the processes governing the acquisition, freedom, or exchange of human chattel mentioned in or important to the text?

R – Religion – This section seeks to create an overview of the religious landscape either mentioned in the text or that provides background for the text. There may be political, economic, social, intellectual, and artistic aspects that create the fiber of the religious structure.

- Where is God in this encounter? In what form is divine presence made known? What is the human response to the divine encounter found in this text?
- What forms of religion are being practiced by the non-Jews or non-Christians in the lesson text?
- What information about Israel or Judaism is needed to understand the passage? (For example, how was the Tabernacle organized?)
- How do practices referenced in the passage foreshadow current Christian practices? Which practices are present in current religious activities (i.e. communion, etc.)? What meaning can be attached to these practices? How are the religious practices mentioned in the text practiced today? How have they evolved?
- What are the attitudes, spiritual dispositions, and behaviors of Jewish or Christian persons in the text?

S – Social – The hierarchy of human interactions serve as the backdrop to many historic accounts. The effort here is to identify not only people but people groups and relationships.

- What is the social status of the people or people groups in the text (i.e., women and children)?
- How are the people or people groups related? What positive or negative interactions are evident?
- What medical issues are prevalent or mentioned in the text? How are people with illnesses treated by others?
- If there are families or familial groups in the text, what are their relationships to one another? To other people?
- What languages and language patterns are prevalent?

I – Intellectual – Learners must consider what intellectual and educational systems are at work within a text.

- What methods of learning or training are mentioned?
- What intellectual or academic discussions or philosophies are included? (For example, how did Paul reason with others about the Scriptures?)
- Are there any philosophical, intellectual, or educational systems or people mentioned? What philosophies and ideologies do they espouse?
- Is there any mention of formal education? What was the content of formal education? Who was provided opportunities for formal education? How are educational systems described? How did they operate?

A – Artistic – The work of artisans, artists, musicians, poets, writers, dancers, and so forth, are important to the culture of any period. Identifying these gives a glimpse into life at the time. The format of the text's construction is also an important artistic point.

- Does the Scripture reference art, dance, music, etc.?
- What artistic elements of poetry and drama are used to create the book or passage under study?
- What phrases are repeated within the text? What metaphors, similes, other comparisons, and contrasts are used to explain concepts?
- Is there a reference to artisan creations such as tools, lamps, furnishings, or clothing? (These were generally forms of art that had practical use in ancient cultures.)

Summary

The Bible has power and purpose. It provides information, inspiration, and declaration of God's existence and power. Its truths undergird our faith. Every Christian should be able to use study tools to unlock the Bible's structure and content. When the Bible is at the center of all congregational teaching, participants take into account the ways in which their encounters with God transform their lives. The study of God's Word provides the knowledge that opens readers' hearts and changes behaviors, attitudes, and spiritual dispositions. The transformative work of Bible-centered teaching involves instructional practices that help learners know who God is, how God cares about their lives and their relationship with Him.

Consider:

1. Create and reflect on a list of Bible passages that have had the most phenomenal impact on your faith journey. Explain why.
2. Develop a plan to model a Bible study strategy in a teaching encounter.
3. Develop a plan to create a class on Bible study strategies.
4. List 10-25 passages of Scripture that you have memorized or would like to memorize. Establish a strategy for doing so or recall how you committed them to memory.
5. Several methods of Bible study are described in this chapter. Select one to investigate more fully.
6. Review the PERSIA model, then practice the strategy using a Bible passage of your choice. Add or modify questions as needed.

CHAPTER SEVEN

Pillar Three: Spirit-Led Encounters

Identifying Encounters

No matter how teachers plan, they cannot know the spiritual needs of participants. Teachers can neither abate nor satisfy a student's longing for God. Addressing spiritual desire requires more than human instinct, teaching skill, and biblical information. Despite how well teachers encourage changes in attitude or suggest options that help students make good choices, the teacher's abilities, charisma, and persuasiveness cannot transform people. Only faith can.

Congregational teaching encounters expect and depend upon the Holy Spirit to act on a learner's faith to make the difference in a learner's life. As Osmer states, "[T]eaching cannot 'cause' faith…. Faith is a free gift from God…. The teaching ministry . . . can and does serve as a special human agency, which God uses to come to persons again and again."[89] Regardless of where congregational teaching occurs, it is Spirit-led when it is executed in faith and with the anticipation of faithful outcomes.

Teachers can nurture faith through their attention to three human variables: the lesson, the teacher, and the learner. These variables are present in every teaching encounter and have the capacity to aid or restrict the teaching process because they impact what is taught and how it is embraced and remembered by learners.

Variable 1: The Lesson

There is no magic formula that yields the perfect lesson every time, but effective Spirit-led lessons include interaction and student involvement in order to stimulate learners' faith. Without these, the lesson simply presents information. Regardless of the topic prayer, reflection, and praxis engage participants' faith and provides Spirit-led instruction.

Prayer

Those who know God are expected to pray; yet, few people instinctively know how to do it. Take the example of a class at a well-known Bible college where all members of the class were either involved in or planning a vocation in church ministry. After taking attendance, the professor randomly asked one of the students present to open the class with prayer. After a prolonged and awkward silence, the professor prayed. The student who refused to pray later admitted that she was terrified of praying in public. It was not a skill she had acquired, and she was uncomfortable with "being put on the spot."

As common as prayer is, it is a skill that must be taught and a discipline that must be practiced. Learners need to know that praying is not begging God to supply a want and does not require flowery language to be heard by God. While worship, praise, confession, and petition are part of prayer, there is no formula for getting it right. Congregational teachers should share Bible passages that help participants learn to pray, understand prayer, and recognize the role of the Holy Spirit as their intercessor. Opportunities for learners to share their requests for prayer, to pray for others, and to share testimonies of answered prayers, allow students to experience the spiritual power of caring.

When Jesus taught the disciples how to pray, He instructed them in the areas they should include in their prayer. The Lord's

Prayer (Matthew 6:9–13) is wonderful, and every Christian should know it by heart. That doesn't mean that it is the only thing we can say to God or that repeating it daily satisfies our desire to seek God's intervention and comfort on specific matters in our lives. In fact, Matthew 6:6–8 records Jesus' explanation that prayer is anchored in our understanding of God, His concern for our well-being, and our relationship with Him. When prayer is incorporated into the learning encounter, it increases participants' faith in God and builds confidence in honoring God's will.

Reflection

Reflection is the process by which one gives careful and serious consideration to an idea, action, or process. It is not abstract thinking. Reflection is focused thinking that unlocks meaning and reveals inner musings on a subject. Scriptures, questions, art, poetry, and more can be catalysts for reflection. Through reflection, learners are able to discern how a given lesson, faith question, or Bible passage applies to their lives.

Because learning styles vary, opportunities for reflection should be varied. Exercises that provide quiet time around focused questions help learners imagine how a Bible passage or biblical concept is relevant in their context. Providing learners with meditation strategies gives them positive approaches to addressing their faith questions. Reflections can be oral, written, or silent. They can be developed in a group, with a partner, or individually. Reflections are not questions to be answered, right or wrong, following a teaching event. They are thoughts, sometimes personal and sometimes incomplete, that learners must decide if they want to share.

When teachers engage writing as a reflection tool, they help learners clarify their thought and identify how it touches their lives. Group discussion that is targeted to address faith questions or biblical content helps learners formulate their concerns and realize that they are not alone in their effort to understand God in their lives. When class members reflect on Scripture and faith, they begin to recognize the work of the Holy Spirit and personally adopt those reflective strategies. When reflections ponder a biblical principle, a personal situation, a social justice topic, or a relevant societal issue participants are able to link their faith to their experiences.

Praxis

It is not enough to simply ask class members to reflect and pray. Their understanding needs to be solidified by putting the skills of spiritual discipline into action. This is called praxis, "the application or use of knowledge or skills."[90] Through praxis, individuals apply what they have learned in order to embrace and utilize the skill and become more open to the messages of the Bible. The class setting can be the starting point for developing and using these skills. In activities of praxis, participants practice praying or challenge themselves to memorize Scripture thus internalizing the importance of memorization and honing memorization strategies. Encouraging participants to share their testimonies of God's deliverance increases faith and fortifies their awareness of divine intervention. As a result, learners gain confidence with sharing the Gospel message in both word and deed. Teaching encounters that engage praxis can encourage learners to use these and other spiritual disciplines such as meditation, fasting, and solitude, on their own in real time and real settings so that learners think differently about their lives, their relationships, their circumstances, and their faith. Through praxis, the Holy Spirit will help learners yield their deepest concerns and daily choices to God.

Spirit-led lessons are characterized by good teaching and faithful execution. Class encounters must be engaging and on point. Well-planned and well-executed lesson experiences create a safe space for students to put their faith into action as they share their concerns, express their opinions, and examine their thoughts about their faith. Incorporating spiritual disciplines does not take away the time planned for teaching the assigned Scripture lesson. Instead, it supplements the lesson. By engaging in praxis, students utilize behaviors that strengthen their spiritual walk. Every class encounter should encourage prayer and reflection as teachers encourage students through concrete applications of their faith. Spirit-led instruction seeks to open learners' hearts to the expectation of faith as an active force in their daily encounters with God, their families, their friends, and the world.

Variable 2: The Teacher

Those who teach for spiritual development and transformation realize that learners must connect the information shared in the encounter to their lives in real ways. Application cannot be dictated by the teacher's actions alone because teachers cannot know the hour when students will suddenly realize that they have gotten past a hurt or are able to manage a situation that was beyond them. Teachers do not know when reflecting on a specific Bible passage will move a learner to faith that is unshakable. They can be assured, however, that it is possible to help learners develop spiritual dispositions that increase their sensitivity to the God-moments of their lives.

The teacher's approach sets the tone for each encounter. When teachers feel that they "know" the Bible (or any assigned topic) and that it is not necessary to spend much time in lesson preparation, they do the students and themselves a disservice. They disrespect the congregation by discounting the ministry they were asked to provide, and they grieve the Holy Spirit by disallowing faith. Lessons by these teachers are usually predictable. They veer off course, leaving the subject of the day and choosing instead to talk about a favorite topic. Learners may leave having had a great fellowship but having gained nothing that nurtures their faith.

Likewise, when teachers focus strictly on the events of the text without discussing the historic context, they restrict the flow of the Spirit in and through those discussions. The spiritual power of the encounter is lost and, again, faith is denied. On the other hand, teachers who attempt to spiritualize the lesson without understanding and incorporating the art and science of teaching and learning also fall short. Both teachers tend to "preach" their ideology rather than help their students reflect on their personal spiritual journeys. The teaching ministry is unique in that it transmits to the intellect the things of the spirit. While teaching can be improved through the use of targeted methods and strategies, the connection of intellect to spirit requires attention. To teach for transformation, teachers must recognize the role of the Holy Spirit in blending human intellect and spirit to generate encounters that transform lives.

The teaching ministry depends on and takes place in an atmosphere of faith because transformation occurs through faith. While congregational teachers hope learners will be awakened to spiritual understanding, faith is the evidence that the teaching is not in vain (Hebrews 11:1). To the passerby, and often to the learners engaged in the lesson, all of this divine energy and expectation looks normal. Even teachers will doubt that they are "getting through" to those before them. That is why faith is so critical. Faith is the confidence that God will provide transformation. It is the proclamation that God is able to do what the Bible promises and describes (Hebrews 1:6). There are two factors that help teachers develop a focus on faith that facilitates Spirit-led teaching: spiritual discipline and the craft of teaching.

Exercise Spiritual Discipline

Reading the Bible is a basic spiritual discipline. Congregational teachers must make Bible reading more than an occasional activity in their own lives. Their Bible reading and study should never be approached as an attempt to amass enough Bible facts to be impressive in a crowd or as a perfunctory devotional effort. Congregational teachers should read their Bibles regularly, even daily, not for the sake of the lesson but for the sake of their own spiritual strength and understanding.

Congregational teachers impact lessons through prayer. Prayer is the teacher's appeal to Almighty God to create a divine encounter. Prayer renders thanks for the transformation that is anticipated and realized. Prayer accounts for how the teaching and learning experience transcends a physical and intellectual encounter to become a transformative experience. Spirit-led teachers don't just develop lesson plans and present creative encounters, they "pray through" lesson preparation. Every aspect of their planning is accompanied by prayer for fresh ideas, effective practices, and meaningful activities. Teachers should pray for students regularly— name-by-name and need-by-need. They should never consider starting or closing classes, excursions, or other learning experiences without having prayer. In fact, they should bathe lesson plans, teaching encounters, and their reflections in prayer so that prayer inundates their lives and the ministry they provide.

Fasting is a spiritual discipline that turns us away from our reliance on physical needs and self-proclaimed abilities. Instead, it confronts us with the reality of God's provision and sustenance as well as our responsibility as persons who claim to love God. Fasting is aimed at a change of attitude by focusing spiritual disposition. Jesus taught that the most important part of the fast is our attitude because it will reflect our spiritual understanding of God's care and provision (Matthew 6:16–21). The prophet Isaiah pointed out that Israel's fasting was not acceptable because they "fast for strife and debate, and to smite with the fist of wickedness: (and) . . . to make your voice to be heard on high" (Isaiah 58:4,). The prophet then explained that the result of fasting should be to do what reflects a focus on what God wants:

> *Free those who are wrongly imprisoned; lighten the burden of those who work for you. Let the oppressed go free, and remove the chains that bind people. Share your food with the hungry, and give shelter to the homeless. Give clothes to those who need them and do not hide from relatives who need your help. (Isaiah 58:6–7, NLT)*

Isaiah's words regarding the acceptable fast identify the spiritual disposition developed through this discipline.

Fasting today can take many forms. Some people fast regularly, even weekly. They choose to focus their time on meditation, prayer, and Bible reading during their abstinence from food and water. Many people practice special types of fasts at specific seasons such as the New Year or Easter. (Denying oneself during Lenten season is another example.) This might include the Daniel Fast, which adheres to the diet of fruits and vegetables described in the Old Testament. Fasting can last from sun up until sun down or for longer periods of time. Sometimes people practice denials by setting aside distracting activities for specific durations. These distractions might include specific foods but may also identify viewing television, using electronics, or surfing social media as distractions from concentrating on spiritual matters. Fasting is a denial of a natural pleasure or activity. During fasting, the natural desire should be replaced with spirit-focused activities such as prayer, Bible reading, meditation, rendering a service, or reading inspirational materials.

Sabbath-keeping as a spiritual discipline causes people to realize how busy schedules and activities hinder their physical, social and spiritual well-being. Sabbath-keeping does not mean acknowledging a particular day of the week as the Sabbath. Instead, it acknowledges the need to take the time to rest and refresh the body, mind, and spirit. The practices of meditation, solitude, and reflection are often part of the Sabbath-keeping process.

There are other disciplines that also heighten teachers' faith. Ephesians 5:19–20 extols the virtues of scriptural affirmations, music, and thanksgiving as disciplines that uplift Christian thinking and refresh the spirit. Philippians 4:8 and Colossians 3:16 provide more specific examples of what should dominate our meditations and thoughts. These spiritual practices open the teachers' hearts to the things of the Spirit and help teachers acknowledge and address their personal struggles to change their attitudes and enhance their spiritual dispositions.

Learn the Craft of Teaching

Specific strategies and educational theories regarding teaching are found throughout this book. Knowing that the teacher is a critical variable in providing Spirit-led instruction should make teachers excited about learning the craft of teaching. Good teachers seek opportunities to know the skill of teaching and welcome critiques regarding their incorporation of learning principles and strategies. Congregational teaching anticipates that lessons and learning experiences will make a difference in what learners gain and how they react. Teachers should be aware of how the research behind teaching and learning helps them appreciate the intricacies with which God has created us. Educational research can teach Christian educators how their actions in the teaching encounter are perceived by the human brain. Teachers should strive to have adequate tools and strategies at their disposal for introducing biblical concepts and focusing learning activities. When teachers depend upon the Holy Spirit to meld their preparation, skill, and artistic efforts, they find that teaching encounters are better able to address the longing and need that God has placed in the learner's heart. (Chapter ten provides an in-depth view of the craft of teaching and its importance to the Christian educator.)[91]

While it is not expected that every Christian educator will seek a degree in education, it is advisable to learn basic elements of teaching. Lesson planning, questioning/thinking strategies, creating a learning environment, encouraging student response, and using creativity and technology in the teaching process are all topics that can and should be explored. Since iron sharpens iron, teachers should consider what they can gain from interactions with congregants who are professional educators or exceptional congregational teachers. Mentoring and networking opportunities with experienced teachers should not be overlooked. In addition, there are many books on congregational teaching that incorporate learning theory and teaching strategies. Videos, conferences, workshops and other learning opportunities may be available through denominations, book publishers, book stores, and online resources. Chapters ten, eleven, and twelve offer additional ideas that extend skills and explore the teaching craft.

Variable 3: The Learner

James Weldon Johnson's poem "Listen, Lord" from his noted work *God's Trombones* is a prayer that includes the line "We come this morning like empty pitchers to a full fountain."[92] Johnson's prayer makes this statement as a plea to God and declares that humans approach God "with no merits of our own." It is a statement of yielding before an Almighty and merciful God written in the style of nineteenth-century Negro preachers who conjured elaborate metaphors in their appeals to God. While Johnson's poetic treatment is still riveting, some people have misappropriated his words. As a result, teachers too often act as though learners come to Christian education classes as "empty pitchers" that teachers are duty-bound to fill. That perception is far from true.

Learners are the third variable in the Spirit-led encounter, and they know why they come to church. Individuals who come to the teaching encounter know who they are and believe that a relationship with God and knowledge of the Bible will enhance their lives. Knowing learner's experiences and expectations can help congregational teachers effectively support the spiritual needs of learners. Christian education programs should strive to create authentic encounters that address learners' lives and needs.

Learners bring different physical, spiritual, social, intellectual, and emotional abilities and concerns to the teaching encounter. Sketches in this chapter provide a glimpse into the general characteristics that can help teachers think about shaping meaningful, Spirit-led encounters that develop learner knowledge, skills, behaviors, attitudes, and spiritual dispositions. While no two people respond in the same way, knowing general characteristics of learners helps in selecting and planning activities, determining materials and resources, and gauging the pace and content of lessons.

There are many resources that provide more in-depth information about individual age groups, but nothing can replace the one-on-one experiences that reveal individual personalities.

A Special Word about Teaching Children

While teachers and churches operate on faith and trust, some guidelines must be adhered to for legal and practical purposes. Every adult who works with children must have a background check. This holds true for young people, from toddlers to teens. In many states this is the law, and in many church insurance policies it is a requirement. In all situations, it is the wise thing to do.

Teachers must make a habit of talking to parents so that sharing concerns is a two-way street. Communication helps parents explain when children are having a bad day or have experienced something that needs special attention. Teachers must know what food or other allergies children have. They should also have contact numbers in case children become ill or need special attention. Communication also helps teachers keep an open door for sharing concerns and giving praise about the learners in their classes.

Children, like adults, are not empty pitchers. Some come from backgrounds and situations that may not have helped them recognize what appropriate behaviors are. Because children are curious and capable of mimicking behaviors (good and bad), teachers and class assistants must be alert at all times. Most children are naturally rambunctious, so adult supervision should be adequate to deter arguments and even bullying.

Teachers should strive to keep all children safe. Classrooms and other areas should follow guidelines regarding their use of space, materials, furniture, and equipment. Cleanliness of cribs, toys, and play areas is a must. Furniture that is appropriate in size and useful for the encounter is also important. Toys and other items must be child friendly to avoid accidents. Both municipal and educational standards should be consulted to make sure that spaces are safe for little ones.

Congregational teachers who work with young children can gain valuable information from reliable Internet sources. The United States Department of Education has published learning targets that can be used to help congregational educators support what children are learning at home or in day care.[93] These learning benchmarks and developmental guidelines can be adapted to help congregational teachers guide children in learning about God and their place in God's love. Teachers can also consult websites that have suggestions on making crafts, selecting music, setting up the learning spaces, and other useful ideas.

Young Children: Birth to Three Years Old

Many churches provide space where children can be active and safe during worship services without disturbing congregants. This type of situation is often viewed as "babysitting." Some local congregations, however, offer formal programs for infants and toddlers that are part of Christian education. Few publishers still develop teaching materials for this age group, but churches that provide those classes realize that little ones are learning in a faith environment. What appears to be playtime is really part of a child's faith formation. Children are learning to trust as they respond to stories, songs, gestures, and instructions. Very young children take in information and use their senses to explore their environment. Toddlers are learning to be comfortable in church settings. Everything youngsters do is an inroad to their learning and their faith journey.

Primary and Early Elementary Learners: Four to Seven Years Old

By age five, a child's personality has developed. When children are ready to enter kindergarten and the early grades of elementary school, they are not just growing in age and height; they are also developing intellectually, socially, emotionally, and spiritually. By this time children have a sense of right and wrong. They know what positive behaviors are and the rewards that come with them. Often, young children equate the Christian education setting with their regular school environment. They view adults as teachers and raising their hands as precursors to responding.

Children in this group have active imaginations. Their understanding of concrete ideas is far beyond their conceptualization of the abstract. For younger learners Jesus, Santa Claus, and the Easter Bunny sometimes feel synonymous. Telling a child that "Jesus lives in your heart" can render visions of a teeny, tiny Jesus, small enough for the human body to accommodate.

Even older children in this group may not understand everything adults think they understand. The story is told about a child who was asked to draw a picture depicting what he learned in class. The child presented a picture of an automobile with three people inside. When the teacher asked him to talk about his picture, the child proudly responded, "That's Jesus driving Adam and Eve out of the Garden!"

The imaginations of young children are their most rich and wonderful learning resources. As their reading, writing, and comprehension skills develop, they can appreciate church-related activities on a concrete level. They can identify baptism and other church rituals. They can explain some characteristics of God related to His nature of love and care, as well as His desire for obedience.

If they have been coming to church all along, children recognize the church as having a special place in their lives. Faith lessons teach children that God loves them. Primary and early elementary learners are ready and usually eager to learn Bible-centered lessons. While age and intellectual development determine how well a child can read, this age group still enjoys following the pictures as they listen to or read about Bible heroes or missions of faith. Musical instruments, physical movement, and play develop a child's sense of worship and wonder. Congregational teachers must be diligent in helping children pray and practice qualities such as respect. They must allow opportunities for children to discover and use their gifts and talents. Guiding children to view such qualities through a framework of faith and service is an important step in faith formation. The congregational teacher can engage children's imaginations, spirits, and intellects through Bible reading and memorable learning episodes.

Juniors and Preteens: Eight to Twelve Years old

As children become juniors or pre-teens, teaching biblical truths with the focus on life lessons is critical. The self-esteem of this group is easily influenced by peers, media messages, cultural icons, and social media (even if they are not allowed to use it). Juniors and preteens are searching to understand where and how they fit in the world. These external influences often gain such prominence in the decision-making process that teachers and parents must struggle to be heard. Ministry activities must contribute to spiritual formation. It is important that students recognize how unique they are to God and the faith community.

Congregational teachers can never assume that they know everything about juniors and preteens. Their bodies are developing rapidly, and their lives are constantly changing. Every day they are faced with decisions related to their self-image and self-worth. For them, it is often more important to be liked by peers—even if these are people they don't know—than to listen to adults who "just don't get it."

Even though teachers may think that children are not paying attention, they are. They recognize fairness, justice, confidentiality, and kindness. Given encouragement, this age group is eager to share their world and "teach" adults what they view as important. Teachers, however, can never attempt to become part of the "in crowd" with these learners. First, that is not authentic; second, it compromises the teacher's ability to provide help in situations that need to be addressed.

When children come from less stable homes or have had some traumatic events in their lives, they often view their choices as limited. Every day, children's decisions are shaping how they respond to the world around them. It is important that teachers not lose focus of what is important in their class interactions. Prominence must be given to the Bible as the key resource in instruction. Discussions of Jesus should focus on Jesus as the giver of life rather than the giver of mandates. As youngsters learn that God cares for them individually and collectively, they will be open to knowing He has a purpose for their lives (Jeremiah 29:11; Colossians 1:9–10).

This age group is eager to know God and the Bible. They enjoy engaging and challenging lessons and competitive activities. They respond to opportunities to memorize Scriptures and serve others because they enjoy being recognized as capable and significant people. That is the way God made them, and congregational teachers should nurture their desire to be included.

Teens: Fourteen to Eighteen Years Old

By the time young people reach their teens, they are facing questions regarding the future of their educational and professional lives. They are entering high school, preparing for college, learning to drive, and learning to take responsibility for their actions. In discussing toddlers, we mentioned their use of senses. For teens, the senses are at a totally elevated level. Hormones rage while interactive and virtual realities abound. Their social interactions go far beyond just knowing the people in their classes or neighborhoods. Technology often defines the way teens interact with the world (literally). It is the means through which they take in information, formulate meaning, and express opinions. It is predicted that by the time young people reach twenty years old, they will have spent 30,000 hours on the Internet and playing video games. (It is not clear if the number of texts sent by that age is even calculable.)

Tapscott, author of *Grown Up Digital*, views the use of technology by young people as a positive action. "This is happening at a time when their brains are particularly sensitive to outside influences, and it has changed their mental reflexes and habits, the way they learn and absorb information."[94] As a result, youth who have been raised in the digital age are far from being less smart. They are better described as people who learn in a different way. They see no need to stockpile information; everything is available on the Internet. There is little reason to memorize telephone numbers or other data; it is available on the smartphone. They may not read as many books, but when they do, they read online or on a tablet. This enables a change in how they read. Need a definition? Touch a word. Turn a page? Scroll down or turn a virtual page. Want to underline or highlight a sentence? Do it electronically and find out how many other people underlined that same sentence!

Teens also have talent—lots of talent. They are capable of being creative and have knowledge of how to do many more things than people give them credit for. Teens also enjoy being introduced to new ideas and exposed to activities that perhaps have not been available in their home or school. When a group of teens were asked to help raise funds for a trip, they wasted no time in meeting the goal. Their plan centered on something they liked—basketball. They organized a three-point shootout contest. They worked with coaches to develop the idea and get equipment. The teens who liked to cook identified the concessions they would sell and prepared it all. Even the teens who were not basketball fans contributed their talents to the project. Teens undertook recruiting the contestants, advertising the event, keeping records of contacts and money collected, preparing the venues and materials, and setting ticket prices. They even identified other promotional items they could make and sell. In the end, they reached their goal and were amazed at their own accomplishment.

At the same time, teen lives are filled with fears. It is no wonder that many teens are on an emotional roller coaster. Stories of bullying, violence, sexual assault, physical temptation, and failure swirl around them and touch their lives far more than adults can imagine. That is why it is important to know the teens in the class and not just the stats on the news. Teen years are fraught with choices, and their world is changing fast. That does not mean, however, that they have decreased in their desire to know God and to be involved in authentic acts of worship and faith. After all, the Bible says to "[t]rain up a child in the way he should go and when he is old, he will not depart from it (Proverbs 22:6). "Old" is more of a reference to maturity than to age. Results may not be seen now, but spiritual maturity is coming!

Because teens live in places of flux and uncertainty, the role of the teen teacher is critical. Teachers of teens must encourage the spiritual development of youth, be authentic in their interactions with them, and model their faith in ways that help these young people navigate the challenges they face. Teachers must ask themselves the hard questions: Is the Bible the center of class life and discussion, or are classes derailed by questions of sex, school, parental problems, and fashion? Does the teacher's presence represent an authentic relationship with God? What direction, assistance, and reassurance of God's plan and purpose for their lives are being provided for teens in each learning encounter (Jeremiah 29:11; Colossians 1:9–10)? Teaching youth provides Christian educators the opportunity to interact with young people at a pivotal time in their lives when they need help embracing their faith.

Adults

The idea that teaching all adults is like teaching any adult makes a faulty assumption. Like children, adults experience various stages in their lives. Those stages come with responsibilities as well as gifts and talents. Young adults are not youth who have grown up. Neither are they in a holding pattern until "maturity" sets in or older people decide they are ready to be given some responsibility. Adult life ranges from the just-graduated and newly employed young adults, to the men and women who are navigating the economic and emotional mindscape of raising a family or living in retirement. Adults who enter the Christian education class will include people who serve as caregivers while negotiating their own issues each day. There will likely be senior adults who are torn between feeling neglected by those who think they are too old to be helpful and feeling helpless because of the unanticipated physical changes that creep in each day.

Adult learners are not a web of woes. Even retirement does

not negate lives well lived. Adults bring rich knowledge of the Bible, their faith, and life. Those who have been in the Christian journey for some time have faith stories to share. Even if they are new converts, adults bring life experiences and creative ideas with them. They are often eager to lend their gifts, talents, personalities, and career or life experiences to the exploration of faith the class is undertaking. The thing that all adults have in common is the fullness of their experiences. They are not empty vessels waiting patiently for the teacher to say a wise word. They are generally wise people eager to engage in meaningful conversation about biblical topics and faithful pursuits. Adults bring the capacity of their brains and the fruits of their lives with them to the congregational setting. Teachers must be mindful to engage them fully and honestly as fellow travelers in the faith walk.

Summary

The aim of Christian education is to transform lives. Spirit-led lessons must explain biblical content and make the heart connection that points students to the Holy Spirit. Showing the Bible's relevance to the lives of learners will create a lasting impression and a faithful response. Teachers must be prepared to pose and respond to life-related questions. This means that teachers must first question themselves. What is the point of the account? In what ways are the people in the Bible similar to the people in your class? What challenges are presented in the lesson? What should learners pray for or seek to understand about their relationship with God and others as a result of the experience you've just shared? This proactive questioning helps teachers relate lessons and experiences to matters of faith.

As much as students enjoy learning biblical facts and reading narrative details, these alone will not result in the transformation teachers seek. Matters of faith need to be uppermost in identifying the purpose of every learning experience. The age level descriptors in this chapter provide only a sketch of each learning group. It takes planning to engage learners in lessons and experiences that point them to

God's presence in their lives. It takes passion to create phenomenal learning through Spirit-led encounters. It takes prayerful engagement to achieve the purpose of congregational teaching: transformed lives.

Consider:

1. This chapter proclaims that a congregational teaching encounter is "Spirit-led when it is performed in faith and with the anticipation of faithful outcomes." Explain why you agree or disagree with that statement.
2. Review the three variables of lesson, teacher, and student.

   a. What additional qualities would you ascribe to each variable?
   b. Are there additional variables that you feel are active in teaching-learner encounters?

3. Select one age category and explain what characteristics you can add to that sketch. Are there any statements that you feel are inadequate or incorrect? Why?

CHAPTER EIGHT

Pillar Four: Authentic Engagement

Keep Teaching Real

Think about this statement: "Don't be so heavenly minded that you're no earthly good."[95] While this statement is critical of Christians who focus on heaven without considering the good they could do for others, it also hides another truism. The call to the teaching ministry requires that our efforts be of "earthly good." We cannot ignore the lives of those we teach. Neither can we disregard the communities and world in which we live. If anyone was heavenly minded, it was Jesus. His ministry included spiritual aspects that only God in human form could perform, like walking on water and raising the dead. But we cannot forget that He also fed the masses, overthrew the tables of the merchants who defiled the Temple, and spoke truth to power as He uplifted the downtrodden and told the gathered crowds they were blessed even in their poverty. In every Gospel account, Jesus was authentic in His understanding of humanity.

The final pillar of congregational teaching, then, is authentic engagement. The people who come to local churches live in real towns and cities. They encounter real struggles and tragedies. Church people are no less impacted by street violence, drug culture, economic downturns, and medical crises than others. Yet, too often the church acts as if it is immune to the plight of the world or points the finger at "the less fortunate" while dismissing as irrelevant the realities of worshipers' lives. The teaching ministry must be authentic in its concern for people if it is to make a difference in individual situations.

Toward Authentic Engagement

Authentic engagement insists that every teaching opportunity insure a real encounter with the life experiences of students. To help with this, instructional design must consider the social realities of learners' lives and respect learners' life experiences. Through lesson encounters, congregational teachers should help learners develop spiritual identities strong enough to navigate their earthly realities. Congregational teaching must be life-focused not because teachers are "trying" to be relevant, but because God *is* relevant and learners need to be assured of that truth. Regardless of learners' ages, every learning experience must aim to help students mature spiritually and embrace the power of the Holy Spirit. This can only be done when the engagement is authentic.

Do What Jesus Did

Jesus did not teach pie-in-the-sky platitudes. He prepared people to face their situations and confront their problems. Congregational teaching must strive to balance its focus on heaven with human attention to earth. People who live in poverty still look to the Gospel to bring a relevant message for their situations and hopes. Those who are more affluent also desire a word that is relevant and encouraging for their circumstances and dreams. It is the responsibility of congregational teachers to allow the Gospel to speak to these varied situations, individuals, and groups equally and simultaneously.

Fortunately, Jesus gave us many examples and a lot of hope. He understood culture and ethnicity. Born and raised in the Jewish tradition, Jesus' ministry demonstrated God's desire that the Gospel genuinely cross cultural, social, ethnic, and economic divides. Jesus recognized that hospitality and authentic engagement would break through barriers. He demonstrated this when He sat with publicans and when He asked a Samaritan woman for water. Jesus' proclamation of justice empowered cultural outcasts. He freed women, children, infirmed individuals, and impoverished persons from the cultural and social bonds of their day. The Good News of Jesus Christ continues to do so even now. Referencing life-related examples allows students to "confront earth with heaven and bring eternity to bear upon time."[96] Instructors who recognize authentic engagement as a pillar of congregational teaching help students confront heaven with their earthly needs and realize the benefit of the Eternal.

Avoid Assumptions and Labels

Christian education cannot develop classes and programs in a vacuum. Neither can teachers produce examples to be placed in a biblical petri dish for students to examine. Unless teachers walk in students' shoes, they are apt to miss the most important aspects of what students face. The teacher who always determines which life issues will be included in the lesson runs the risk of accusing all youth of being sexually active (or about to be) and complaining that all young adults are careless with their finances. Making assumptions about who learners are and what they think mislabels and insults participants while distracting from lesson concepts. Christian teaching is incomplete and ineffective if learners are not given opportunities to discuss their realities. Participants must be able to identify how their lives are impacted by their encounters with the Holy Spirit through the Bible and congregational teaching. The wise teacher guides class members to self-identify issues that are relevant to the discussion.

Avoid labeling learners. The tendency to see people as shy, talkative, disengaged, or unresponsive does a disservice to the learner and the class. When learners are categorized, teachers tend to not involve them or involve them at the expense of ignoring other class members. The truth is that we cannot know if our assumptions are correct. Teachers err when they accuse learners of not being open during discussions or try to force participants to be "honest" about their feelings or what they are facing. Emotional wounds are created when participants confide in a teacher only to find that their situation has become the basis for the next lesson. The wounds of individual learners do not heal easily. In fact, they can fester, and as a result, teachers' methods can either stymie spiritual growth or run participants away from the local assembly. It is best to concentrate on creating an authentic atmosphere of safety and transparency that fosters freedom to communicate about faith and life. Encounters must assure students that their emotional, physical, and psychological needs are addressed with genuine concern and Christian care.

Acknowledge and Address Bias

Ethnicity, community, family, socio-economic realities are all contributing factors to our social identities. Some people would have us believe that we live in a post-racial world. The truth is that differences—racial and non-racial—exist. While some churches have either made a conscious effort to be diverse in their membership or been blessed to have broad appeal, the inclusiveness of congregations is still lacking. Martin Luther King Jr.'s criticism of eleven o'clock Sunday morning as the most segregated hour in the country still holds merit nearly sixty years later. Our nation is fraught with tension, polarization, and selective discrimination. King's beloved community is not yet a reality even in places of worship. Because of this, churches and Christian education programs must be mindful to welcome everyone regardless of differences. It is difficult to enjoy the fellowship of a congregation when you are the only "other" person or family in the sanctuary, and every turned head points that out.

Christian education must guard against allowing insensitivity and bias to creep into its instructional encounters. When learning materials used by children of poverty only include examples of affluence, those children run the risk of resenting their family's struggles. If single adults are bombarded with hints that marriage is the only "complete" status one can have, their spiritual development may be challenged. Similarly, efforts at diversity that include inaccuracies or stereotypes are off-putting. Spirit-led encounters must be inclusive. They can only be authentic when participants are welcomed and allowed to share their realities and experiences as part of the dialogue.

Consider Attitudes and Accommodations

At its most basic level, the teaching ministry is concerned with instruction in scriptural literacy. Because congregational teaching encounters often remind people of their school-based learning experiences, congregational teachers should be mindful of how memories of school days long gone or current educational engagement shape the congregational setting. Those emotional realities can hinder or help learners to be open to the work of the Holy Spirit in the instructional setting of the church. People who enjoyed school and found it easy to navigate may enjoy activities that are rich in conversation, intellectual pursuit, and additional reading or writing tasks. People who don't have fond memories of school are not likely to appreciate a reminder at church. Children that struggle with learning or acceptance by their school peers may have difficulty with the teaching environment at church if it has a similar aura. Because of their prior experiences, learners need multiple avenues to help them process teaching encounters.

Physical realities cannot be overlooked or minimized. Most churches attempt to equip learning spaces with appropriately sized chairs and tables for youngsters. In small or less affluent congregations, that may not be possible. What may also get lost is the need for large crayons and pencils that small hands can use. The availability of safe scissors, learning toys, and proximity to washrooms is important to creating a friendly space and experience for the youngest learners.

The needs of learners who are physically challenged are often ignored unless adults or families bring them up. While most US cities require handicap accessible buildings, many churches were built prior to those laws or have just not found adequate or affordable ways to retrofit their facilities. Other churches have just not been creative or attentive to developing accessible and comfortable sacred spaces for learning. When classes are held only on the second floor of a facility without an elevator, lift, or ramp, wheelchair-bound congregants are excluded from participation. Many a class trip has left faithful members without a way to participate simply because the bus was not wheelchair accessible.

Adults and children with hearing or vision impairments may stay away from congregations because they really do not have access that others take for granted. Families with children who have special needs have difficulty finding churches that recognize and accommodate their situations. The issue of physical realities is not totally about accessibility. Room arrangements, voice projections, lighting, cluttered slides, indecipherable handouts, and distracting activities in close proximity to the learning space are all indications that physical realities and needs have been ignored. Sometimes these exclusions are blamed on financial lack, but when the root is found to be attitudinal, the problem is much worse. Learners' spiritual enlightenment is distracted when their physical engagement is compromised.

Recognize Individuality
Teachers who regularly rely on the Holy Spirit for guidance will incorporate strategies, activities, and projects that seek to help learners do more than cope on a daily basis. These teachers plan encounters in order to help learners see the salvation of the Lord in the context of their lives. Learners want to know how to "set their affection on things above" (Colossians 3:2), and teachers must plan lessons that help them do that. This requires teachers to take into

account the emotional, physical, and learning style realities each individual brings to the teaching-learning encounter.

Spirit-led, Bible-based, authentic teaching aims to equip individual members with the tools to discover and apply biblical truths to their individual situations. The ways in which people of any age learn are called their learning styles. (Chapter ten explores these in greater detail.) Acknowledging learning styles provides authentic avenues for addressing learning differences and individualities. The style of learning engaged by any student provides a window into how he or she makes meaning of the content of the teaching-learning experience. Some people process information through reading, writing, listening, or speaking. Others appreciate the logical progression of how information is presented. Personal learning style also accounts for how individuals see biblical principles intersecting human need. Some learners make the connections when visual cues such as art, charts, photos or graphs are presented. (Indeed, a picture is worth a thousand words.) Wise teachers, therefore, pray for guidance about how to vary presentation styles, knowing that the Holy Spirit will use their efforts to provide authentic and meaningful learning experiences for each student.

Reveal Spiritual Identities

People seek God because the Holy Spirit has given them the faith to do so. Their faith activates spiritual dispositions and opens the door to spiritually teachable moments where learners can craft and affirm their spiritual identities. People come to church with various backgrounds and religious experiences. No one enters the sanctuary doors "religion free," even if they have never been to church or seen a Bible. For some people, the Bible may have never been read or considered to be a resource for living. For others, the practices of worship or the style of preaching in one church may give them comfort while another congregation's worship style makes them nervous. People come to Christian education encounters with experiences and preconceived ideas that identify who they are and the relationship they seek with Jesus Christ. It is this perception of their relationship with Christ that gives them a spiritual identity. This identity becomes the platform upon which their character and vision will be aligned with the Holy Spirit.

One factor impacting a learner's spiritual identity is his or her emotional need. Congregational teachers should give ear to the pain and passions of their students of all ages. This does not mean that learners expect teachers to "solve" problems. When congregational teachers' attitudes project a desire to "fix" people or situations, teachers have stepped out of bounds. At the same time, teachers should not ignore or shy away from learners or hide behind the Bible when confronted with often subtle, but sometimes raw, concerns or actions that indicate hurt. The opening of "The Serenity Prayer" can help teachers and learners put things into perspective:

God grant me the serenity
To accept the things I cannot change;
Courage to change the things I can;
And wisdom to know the difference.

Authentic encounters that are Spirit-led help participants know that while they cannot change what has happened, they can look to God and the Bible to develop the spiritual tools for coping and changing what they can. Spirit-led teaching, therefore, must help students acquire wisdom. "The Lord gives wisdom; from his mouth come knowledge and understanding" (Proverbs 2:6). The spiritual journey is a lifelong endeavor. How well and how quickly persons develop the spiritual DNA that strengthens them cannot be calculated. For that reason, teaching encounters must allow space for authentic engagement that helps learners recognize their spiritual identities.

Congregational teaching seeks to help learners recognize how knowing God through the Bible provides a sense of identity that is anchored in Christian purpose. In a world where media messages and social media interactions often dictate one's self-worth, developing and strengthening spiritual identity requires more than superficial efforts to make people feel good. As part of the body of Christ, we are adopted into the purpose of God for our lives and our world. Congregational teaching accentuates spiritual purpose. Scriptural affirmations such as "I can do all things through Christ which strengthens me" (Philippians 4:13) encourage learners to see the power of Christ at work in their lives.

Connected to self-worth is our tendency to equate self-esteem with achievement and success. News articles, television programs, and magazines tout the lifestyles of athletes and celebrities as not only attainable but also as norms of success. For learners of varied ages, the acquisition of material wealth is viewed as the standard for attainment. Such distorted visions of "the way life is" can rob people of hope when such dreams and expectations are not met. The societal bar for achievement is tenuous. Gaining a sense of worth through the fickle changes of cultural standards is difficult at best and meaningless in the long run.

It is natural to seek approval from family, friends, and society at large. Our spiritual identities, however, demand that we look elsewhere for our sense of self-worth. Jesus' words in Matthew 6:33 ring loud and clear here: "But seek ye first the kingdom of God, and his righteousness; and all these things shall be added unto you." The richness of the Bible texts and the actions of the Holy Spirit are able to satisfy our natural craving for achievement, success, and acceptance. True self-worth is developed when students recognize how their "natural" aspirations to succeed are addressed through biblical and spiritual avenues.

Finally, spiritual identity is shaped by encounters with the Holy Spirit. That is why being Spirit-filled is the prerequisite encounter in the process of being Spirit-led. The Spirit of God dwells in us, and the Comforter teaches us what we are to do and say (John 14:16–17, 26). How can the Holy Spirit lead someone who has not connected to the Holy Spirit? Being born-again is critical to having an identity in Christ (John 3:3). This is not an argument about denominational understandings of what "born-again" means. Whether the congregation is Pentecostal or Baptist, Reformed or Catholic, or anything within or outside of those designations is irrelevant. Spirit-led teaching anticipates that participants will have an encounter with the Holy Spirit that will give them an identity as a Christian.

Without authentic engagement, the individuals in congregational classrooms will either struggle to retro-fit a view of God that includes them or walk away from these encounters devoid of hope and vision. Relevance is not a byword; it is a mainstay of congregational teaching that seeks to help learners recognize their spiritual ID. Without life-related examples, Noah is still in the flood and Sampson is still facing Goliath. The fact is that Jesus is no longer on the Cross. Jesus' prayer in John 17 was "not only for these disciples but also for all who will ever believe in me through their message" (John 17:20, NLT). Jesus prayed that each believer would have an identity in Him. Generations of believers were included in that prayer, which gives us comfort and allows us to venture into our lives with confidence that Jesus continues to make intercession for us (Romans 8:24).

Summary
Christian education programs stand on the front line with a Gospel message that addresses the genuine needs of those who seek to develop their faith in God. Authentic engagement does not mean every lesson is plagued with woes and moans. It does mean every encounter provides instruction that gives preference to the Bible and its power to develop attitudes and spiritual dispositions learners need in the everyday encounters of their lives. In this way, learners develop a spiritual identity that helps them navigate their world.

Because congregants want to understand how to live out their faith in the world, congregational teachers must help them through actions of love, compassion, and community. Each encounter must help students see themselves as children of God. Congregational teachers must assure learners that God's direction is clear in His Word and that the Bible is an authentic voice even in their wilderness experiences. Regardless of the realities learners bring to the encounter, congregational teachers must use their heads and hearts in designing learning experiences that are authentic and engaging. The following advice, incorrectly attributed to Saint Francis of Assisi, provides an excellent framework for doing this: "Preach the Gospel always, and when necessary, use words."[97] Exhibiting love, engaging in honest conversation, and enjoying the company of the assembled believers will "preach" a message that welcomes each learner regardless of age, stage, or experience. When congregational teachers authentically engage learners through Bible-centered, Spirit-led learning encounters, students have assurance in God's plan for their lives.

Consider:

1. Several concerns were raised in this chapter under the heading "Toward Authentic Engagement." Respond to one or more of the sub-headings by identifying where and if these challenges and opportunities are present in your congregation.
2. This chapter urges teachers to recognize individuality in learners. What approaches do you think can best help teachers reach this goal?
3. Who are you? Write a description of your spiritual identity.
4. What benefit is gained when teachers articulate their spiritual identities? Is there a benefit for the teacher's interactions with learners?
5. This section identified five features and four pillars as foundations for the transformative work of Christian education. How would you summarize the importance of these foundations?

SECTION THREE

CORE: An Approach to Sustainable Teacher Preparation

Shew me thy ways, O Lord; teach me thy paths. Lead me in thy truth, and teach me: for thou art the God of my salvation; on thee do I wait all the day. Psalm 25:4-5

Give instruction to a wise man, and he will be yet wiser: teach a just man, and he will increase in learning. Proverb 9:9

Why CORE?

If the church is called to elevate the teaching ministry, then teachers must be prepared to step up to its challenges and triumphs. If local churches are to move congregational teaching from the margins of church life to the center of the church's ministry, then teachers cannot be left to "figure it out" on their own. "Quickie" workshops and one-time events can be useful but will not fully do the job. Preparing congregation members to serve in the teaching ministry means equipping teachers with appropriate knowledge, skills, and behaviors. Teacher preparation should strengthen attitudes and spiritual dispositions. This section details CORE, a comprehensive model for ongoing and sustainable teacher preparation.

CORE is an acronym for the four areas of teacher preparation: Call, Orientation, Refining, and Enrichment. Many congregational teacher preparation programs focus on the practical, skill-driven aspects of teaching. They identify learner needs in order to help potential teachers create objectives and identify strategies for classroom instruction. While these are critical skills, CORE advocates a different approach. **Call** begins the preparation process by helping teachers identify their own spiritual journeys and the source of their commitment to teach. **Orientation** takes Christian educators into the basics of teaching as they identify or affirm their area of service. **Refining** is the process through which teacher knowledge, skills, and abilities are enhanced. **Enrichment** guides teachers to explore their growing capacity for leadership and service to the teaching ministry and the church. The CORE approach to sustainable teacher preparation provides a framework that local churches can adopt or adapt for their congregations.

CHAPTER NINE

C – Call: Recognizing the Call

Called to Purpose

Teacher preparation begins with an understanding of why people are part of the teaching ministry; therefore, the C, or Call portion, of CORE focuses on four areas:

- The call to faith in God through the sacrifice of Jesus Christ
- The call to a community of believers
- The call to spiritual transformation
- The call to serve God and the church

The Call to Faith

The Greek word for "call" is *kaleo,* meaning "a divine invitation to participate in the blessings of redemption."[98] We are called when we are enlisted by the Holy Spirit "to share in God's intentions."[99] The general call to salvation is accepted when we acknowledge Christ as Savior in response to the saving grace of God. It is then that we realize God has invited us into a special, spiritual relationship to which we have no other claim or credentials. In Romans, Paul asserts that the Gentiles in Rome (and all Christians) are called to "belong to Jesus Christ" as "his own holy people" (Romans 1:6, NLT). Those who claim the name "Christian" also claim to be "the called" of God.

This divine invitation goes beyond membership in a church or a local assembly. It is a *personal* invitation from Almighty God. We are not invited and then left wandering on our own to determine the point of it all. God has called us to be in relationship with Him (Romans 8:14–16), a relationship that is not based on any worthiness we might think we have. In fact, we are called to relationship despite our existence in spiritual darkness. It is from this state of alienation that God calls us into "His marvelous light" (1 Peter 2:9). Second, God does not call us from darkness to a void, but from darkness to "all things that pertain to life and godliness" (2 Peter 1:3). In essence, God invites us to fully abandon our spiritually dark state and fully embrace the glory and virtue of His kingdom.

From our human perspective, we are humbled by the loftiness of God's invitation and the hopelessness of our human efforts. The realization that we are incapable of maintaining this relationship or even functioning in relationship with the Almighty without His intervention leads us to worship God and seek His guidance for how to please Him. Those who become congregational teachers should understand not only that Christ died but also that His death was substitutionary for them. This needs to be more than an intellectual assumption; teachers need to believe in Jesus as Savior.

Those who desire to enter the teaching ministry must do so with full assurance that they have accepted the call to faith. In many denominations, the call to faith is a formalized ritual of childhood. Perhaps the pastor or designees are tasked with providing initial religious instruction either through confirmation classes, Sunday school participation, or special Bible studies designed to guide children and youth to a life of faith. Faith is then reinforced through worship experiences, special observances (such as Christmas and Easter), fellowship gatherings, and other congregational events and activities. The assumption is that church involvement will increase one's faith in God, but we cannot be certain. What is certain is that the call to faith is multifaceted. For teachers, acknowledging their call to Christian life is the first step in Christian service.

The Call to Community

In 1 Corinthians 1:9, Paul declares that "God is faithful, who has called you into fellowship with his Son, Jesus Christ our Lord." Paul relates "God's faithfulness" to our "Christian fellowship" in verse 10. Thus, Paul states his desire that Christians "live in harmony with each other. Let there be no divisions in the church . . . be of one mind, united in thought and purpose" (NLT). This call to community is predicated upon the acceptance of the call to faith. It is not just a call to a local assembly, but it is a call to human relationships that are centered in our common spiritual connection to Jesus Christ. Our unity is based on our faith in God and the power of the Holy Spirit to unify and unite us as Christians.

We want to assume that anyone who volunteers to participate as a teacher or worker in the Christian education ministry has an attitude of cooperation, collaboration, and helpfulness. But sometimes people decide to teach for reasons that are contrary to the call to community. There are those who seek the opportunity to become congregational teachers for prestige. They view teaching as a status symbol in their search for popularity or purpose. They may place teachers at the top of the Christian education ladder while students and those who facilitate administrative needs are a little less worthy in the kingdom. Others seek the position of teacher in the belief that it will give them the appearance of being spiritually strong. Their concern is not that they are able to share the Gospel with others, but that they are viewed as members of an organization with whom God is well pleased.

Another source of disunity is found when teachers fail to embrace the practices of their faith tradition. While questions regarding faith and tradition are legitimate, the congregational classroom is not the place for teachers to argue with the church. It is important that teachers understand how faith practices are related to the Bible and developed through spiritual formation. Teaching carries a commitment to the church community and the tenets of faith. Teachers need to know the history and beliefs of their tradition because their responsibility is to teach the Word of God on behalf of their specific faith community.

CORE training aims to help potential teachers discern their spiritual well-being as members of the faith community. When teachers recognize their call, they also examine their motives for involvement in the ministry. Christian education leaders must prayerfully seek to alleviate problems that stem from misplaced motives or misunderstandings of mission. Leaders are to help teachers "live in harmony with each other" guarding against "divisions in the church" and strengthening unity of "thought and purpose" (1 Corinthians 1:9). Throughout the CORE training, but especially during the Call phase, leaders must create opportunities for shared discussions about the purpose of service and the passion that undergirds our call. Reflections, meditations, even outside assignments must keep the concept of community in the forefront. When teachers recognize their call to community, they understand that those who teach in the church are there to guide others into the faith.

The Call to Spiritual Transformation

Teachers are not only expected to help others realize spiritual transformation, but also they are called to be transformed in their lives as well. Transformation in teachers' lives is cultivated through their personal Bible-centered and Spirit-led encounters. A teacher who neglects personal Bible study is a teacher whose lessons are soon bereft of depth. They rely on platitudes and social commentary in hopes of spurring spiritual growth. Throughout the CORE process, leaders should be aware of aspiring teachers who need additional Bible knowledge. Without this foundation, their teaching will not be successful, and their own spiritual lives will suffer.

Spiritual transformation should be evident in teachers' attitudes and spiritual dispositions. Attitudes change all the time, but teachers should demonstrate respect for the ministry and the students. Their conversations and associations should be positive regarding their interest in Christian education. Spiritual disposition refers to the openness of teachers to receive the things of the Spirit, and to discern and anticipate that God is at work in their lives. When teachers recognize their call to transformation, they anticipate that the Holy Spirit will be active in the planning, execution, and outcome of the lessons they teach. These teachers are willing to seek God through prayer for their preparation, their teaching efforts, and the lives of their students. Christian educators who realize the call to spiritual transformation know that they are not the last word in transformative teaching. God is.

The Call to Serve God and the Church

The Call to serve is the call to vocation. Every local assembly has a process for engaging converts and new members into the life of the congregation. It is likely that this process includes helping members identify themselves as part of the church family. In some congregations, this process is embedded into the church culture and provides opportunities for congregants to discern their personal call and gifts. For others, the process involves simply asking members to select a ministry or auxiliary that appeals to them. Too often, however, the process does not help congregants explore their personal faith journeys as a platform for discerning their area of service. Once we have accepted the offer of salvation, God calls us to serve on earth as citizens in the divine kingdom. This is the "vocation to which we are called." As Frederick Buechner has said, "The place God calls you to is the place where your deep gladness and the world's deep hunger meet."[100] Believers are "called according to his purpose" (Romans 12:28).

The Holy Spirit prepares us to benefit the body of Christ through the gifts Christ has bestowed for that purpose. In order for our actions to produce the results God expects and demands, we must operate in His grace, through His gifts, and by His power in specific areas of service. When we recognize the divine nature of God's call, we embrace the vocation or work as our reasonable service (Romans 12:1)

Like the call one accepts to the ordained ministry of the modern church, one's call to serve in the teaching ministry must first be acknowledged by the person who is called. Without this admission of a call to serve, teaching becomes a social activity that arranges opportunities for groups of people to gather—with or without a Bible in the room! Whether they teach children, youth, or adults, teachers must acknowledge and accept the responsibility of the call to serve through the teaching ministry. This call must be confirmed and nurtured by church leaders in order for teachers to develop the knowledge and skills they need to teach others.

Finally, the call to serve through teaching must be celebrated. Like ordination services in which the entire congregation or faith community celebrates one's call to ministry, the call to teach should be affirmed and celebrated by the local congregation. Celebration, however, means more than throwing a party as the culminating act of a "training class." Celebration means recognizing the importance of the teaching ministry. It means acknowledging the value of biblical teaching. It means embracing the teachers who prepare the people of God to walk in faith. It means that churches must *Elevate the CORE* so that all members will find their place of ministry or service according to the power that works in them.

Classes in the Call phase of CORE must include at least an introduction to the spiritual disciplines as a way of life. Through Call, teachers should learn to embrace spiritual disciplines as routines of their own faith. They must be challenged to apply biblical principles to their personal issues so that they can model this to others. Call classes should also offer teachers the opportunity to take a spiritual gifts inventory to help discern and affirm teaching as their area of ministry service. During Call, an introduction to the teaching ministry will help prospective teachers honestly consider church expectations and their responsibilities in teaching.

Summary

We are called of God for God's purpose. Therefore, CORE training begins with our calls to faith, community, spiritual transformation, and service. By beginning teacher preparation with the four program elements of Call, the teacher's salvation story becomes the catalyst for serving in the church. Thus, the transition to the Christian education ministry is made by congregants who can articulate their identities as Christians, recognize their ministry gifts, and make a responsible commitment to serve. CORE is more than training in teaching skills. It is also a pathway to spiritual development for those who embark on this journey of learning.

Consider:

1. The Call phase of CORE training identifies four areas: (a) the call to faith, (b) the call to community, (c) the call to transformation, and (c) the call to serve. Record your reflections on each of these aspects of your Christian call.
2. Two examples of disunity and misplaced motives are listed in this chapter. Do you agree with these assumptions? Why?
3. Several ideas for fostering unity are presented under "Call to Community." What can you add to this list?
4. How do you connect the calls to faith and transformation to teacher's call to serve?
5. How would you describe your congregation's story of faith? Can the four areas of Call be related to your congregation's story?
6. What do you see as the greatest benefit of the Call phase of the CORE Teacher Preparation Program?

CHAPTER TEN

O – Orientation: Exploring the Teaching Process

The Journey to Teach

In designing Orientation classes, each church has to determine how long the sessions will last, the guidelines and standards, and the expected outcomes. If a solid introduction to the teaching ministry was not provided during Call, it should be done at the beginning of the Orientation phase. Classes in CORE training can accommodate potential, novice, and experienced teachers. Therefore, the design of the classes should anticipate a range of abilities and needs.

Some attendees will have formal educations that have prepared them to teach. Most will have career, volunteer, or life experiences that help them navigate and appreciate the tasks of teaching. While all of these people have kind hearts and good intentions, few will possess all of the skills to teach effectively for transformation. Local congregations must be prepared to help participants stretch their knowledge, skills, and abilities for service in Christian education.

Orientation classes highlight teaching strategies and provide training in how to use them in congregational settings. Those participants who are just entering the teaching ministry will begin to practice the art and science of teaching. Current teachers will hone their skills for transformative teaching. Even if participants are professional educators, they will gain a fresh perspective of teaching as ministry.

While Orientation will include skill development, it is also a time of discernment. Sessions must provide a platform for discussion of participants' anxieties about teaching. As concerns regarding each person's skill development, Bible knowledge, or faith journey surface, prayer and reassurance of ongoing support are needed. The design of Orientation classes must incorporate an atmosphere where these issues can be addressed.

Orientation incorporates five distinct but interrelated units of study:

- Using Resources and Tools
- Engaging the Brain and Spirit
- Addressing Learners' Needs
- Putting It All Together
- Helping Teachers Find their Place in the Ministry

After successful completion of the Orientation program, participants are ready to begin or enhance their role as Christian educators.

Using Resources and Tools

While some faith traditions believe that scholarship and Bible study are mutually exclusive activities, it cannot be assumed that seeking understanding with the aid of theological commentaries will lessen one's love for God. A teacher's Bible study serves as personal spiritual enhancement and as background for lesson preparation. A teacher's personal library should include Bibles, biblical and theological references, and teaching resources. It can be physical, virtual, or a combination of the two. As teachers explore materials and resources, they will find the list is endless.

Bibles and Extra-Biblical Resources

A personal study library should contain both devotional and study Bibles. Many of the popular Bibles available today are devotional. These resources provide a basic understanding of how the Scriptures touch our lives and encourage spiritual maturity. Devotional Bibles may focus on specific populations such as women or men, teens or children. They may also address the interests of specific groups such as veterans or athletes. In study Bibles, each book begins with an essay written by the theologian who translated the text and provided the commentary. They may include research-based references and footnotes as well as concordances and indexes. Charts or articles on biblical, historical, and cultural information are common.

Both devotional and study Bibles come in several translations. Hebrew and Chaldee are the original Old Testament languages, while the New Testament was written in biblical Greek. Since teachers are not expected to know the original language of Bible passages, translations begin to address this issue. The King James (KJV) and New King James (NKJV) versions are common and preferred by some denominations. The New International Version (NIV) is the basis of many modern Bible publications and materials and has become a mainstay in many congregations. Other translations such as the New Living Translation (NLT) stay close to the original meaning but attempt to provide more modern language. The *Common English Bible* is perhaps one of the latest translations to be underwritten by a denomination; it makes an effort to combine scholarly and devotional materials for today's readers.

Some Bibles are paraphrases, not translations. *The Message Bible*, *The Living Bible*, and the *Amplified Bible* fall into this category. They offer a summary of the text without considering the original language. Translations and paraphrases are helpful for understanding— in plain English—what the Scriptures say. The Bible Gateway, an online resource, identifies forty-six English translations and versions.[101] One's choices are definitely based on personal preference and purpose.

Teachers must acquire the skill to use extra-biblical texts and reference materials that open the door to independent Bible study. While study Bibles may contain resources, teachers may find a need to learn more. Bible dictionaries, encyclopedias, concordances, atlases, topical Bibles, commentaries, lexicons, and other resources can provide help for teachers who desire to know more about specific words, historical context, or the original language and intent of passages.

Technology has made it possible for anyone to conduct an in-depth Bible study electronically. Many software packages and apps provide entire libraries of Bibles, commentaries, and reference materials. Websites such as Bible Gateway are free and offer access to an abundance of resources. Public and theological libraries will prove helpful as well.

Teaching Tools

Manipulatives or objects are helpful in bringing the biblical text to life. These are physical materials that can be touched and handled in class. They help learners' engage in discussion, understand Bible passages, and retain information. Teaching tools include electronic and physical resources. It is common to use objects with small children because children learn and make sense of the world through play. But object lessons can be used with learners of every age. Incorporating these tools helps students "see" and experience the events and concepts that are being explored. Pieces of fabric or replicas of Roman coins will enhance the understanding of New Testament passages. Displaying a model of Herod's Temple as the class discusses Jesus and the money changers creates a powerful teaching moment at any age. Using a hymn or modern worship song developed from a psalm makes the poetry and music of the Psalms meaningful.

When teachers keep their eyes and imaginations open to the creative use of objects, lessons can take on new dimensions. A lesson on Amos 7 taught by a building contractor using a plumb line as a visual created a never-forgotten lesson for every adult in the room!

When several women committed to teach a Bible study to incarcerated teen girls, they soon found that the inmates lacked the literacy skills to read the biblical text or use the curriculum materials. The teachers used the *Visual Bible*, a video that combines live action with word-for-word NIV translation, as the solution. The combination of video, audio, and print also improved comprehension skills. The young women were able to identify the message of the Bible text, explain how it was applicable to their unique situation, and recognize the hope it gave them for life after release. They were engaged and grateful that Scriptures were accessible to them.

Teachers can always be encouraged to find materials on their own or to use their imaginations to enhance the lesson. The Christian Education Department, however, must give guidelines on what is appropriate and available. Does the church have the resources to supply copies? Which classrooms have white boards? Are projectors and computers available for PowerPoint and other displays? Does the church provide access to the Internet? Some teachers and classes use Facebook, but the church should be aware of this. For some groups, social media use may need parental consent. In almost any class today, youth and adults will use telephones and tablets as part of their materials. Christian education should help teachers make the most of these innovations.

Engaging the Brain

Spirit-led lessons are impactful because God has wired us to receive information on physical, emotional, mental, and spiritual levels. Science is constantly revealing more about how fearfully and wonderfully we are made (Psalm 139:14). Knowledge of how the brain functions sheds light on what teachers can do to engage learners of all ages. Today, we know a great deal about how the brain helps learners make sense of and respond to stimuli.

The brain's *occipital lobe* is responsible for vision. This is the area that processes visual information and creates understanding about patterns and spatial order. Because of the occipital lobe, the incorporation of pictures, images, and models are more than just interesting decorations to the learning space. Calculation and language are two of the processes that occur in the *parietal lobe*. This area is also credited with rendering insight and inspiration as well as our feelings of satisfaction and pleasure. Speech and listening, creativity and judgment, memory and voluntary movement occur through the *temporal and frontal lobes.* The temporal lobe also links current situations with past occurrences and helps us identify relevance. The *cerebellum* in the lower region of the brain controls our movements and some of our cognitive skills. The *amygdala* and *hippocampus* are largely responsible for our emotional reactions.[102]

Every cell in the brain contributes to what we learn because electronic impulses create activity in the dendrites of brain cells. Researchers once thought it was impossible to learn new ideas and concepts after a certain age. We know now that our brains continue to make connections well into adulthood. With all of this going on at once, it is no wonder that the brain also requires quiet time in order to process what occurs in the classroom. Effective teachers learn to use the art of reflective activities and the science of engaging learners to trigger memory and help learners connect teaching encounters with their life experiences.[103] Because our brains continue to process social situations and retrieve information and memories long after the teaching is done, the brain cannot be overlooked as a key reason we experience teaching as phenomena.

Five Paths to Learning and Application

Transformative learning does not occur accidentally. The brain is constantly working, but teachers must create meaningful stimuli in order to optimize retention and application. There are many theories about what works. This section presents five paths that help all teachers at all levels: **Learning Styles, Multiple Intelligences, Organizational Learning, Age-Level Learning,** and **Inductive Study and Questions**. While they are presented separately, it is not difficult to see how these paths are related.

Learning Style

Infusing visual, auditory, and tactile stimuli into instruction helps learners process the activities and events under study. Visual learners make sense of written words as well as pictures and images. They need to see or read information to get the most from the learning experiences. Some students are auditory learners. This means they glean the most through hearing and speech. They are particularly open to hearing others and exchanging ideas. Social interactions as well interactions through group work helps auditory learners clarify meaning and apply the discussions to their lives. Tactile learners use motion and touch as part of their learning process. They might enjoy games or be prone to express themselves through hand gestures. These learners relate to a subject best through interactions and object lessons. Tactile learning is not reserved for children who enjoy touching objects or playing with blocks and clay. Adults also enjoy hands-on experiences and appreciate handling artifacts.

There is no "one size fits all" approach. A prolonged lecture is not likely to enhance the spiritual encounter for those not prone to auditory learning. A class that focuses extensive time on the printed page can be a turn-off for tactile learners. "Round robin" reading is an activity where individuals are asked to take turns reading passages. For the adult or child who has difficulty reading, this can be painful or embarrassing. Classes should balance lecture with visual and auditory cues. The integration of both electronic and print media add energy to a class. Alternating group work with reflective exercises increases the opportunities for retention and spiritual application. Teachers who go overboard and jump from activity to activity cause confusion. Prayerful attention to variety and moderation are keys to addressing students' learning styles.

Multiple Intelligences

New theories about learning are discovered regularly. However, some older learning theories couple well with the latest research in brain-based learning. These theories give congregational teachers insight on how they can spark transformative learning. In 1983, Dr. Howard Gardner of Harvard University proposed the Theory of Multiple Intelligences. Gardner, who saw IQ as a narrow and non-descriptive concept, referred to each "human intellectual competence" as an "intelligence."[104] For Gardner, these intelligences are reactions of the human brain and represent "the ability to resolve problems or create products, that are valued within one or more cultural settings."[105] When people are extremely gifted in these areas, we understand exactly why each is categorized as an "intelligence." We may even refer to people as geniuses in an area (musical genius, math genius, etc.). Over the years, Gardner and other researchers have added to and refined his ideas. In fact, Garner states clearly that there "can never be a single, irrefutable and universally accepted list of human intelligences."[106] Nevertheless, Gardner's theory provides insight into how each of these intelligences contributes to learning.

- *Linguistic intelligence* utilizes reading and writing as well as speaking to make sense of information.
- *Logical-mathematical intelligence* gives preference to numbers and logical progressions in the thinking process.
- *Spatial intelligence* employs pictures, artistic depictions as well as the spatial arrangement of items and design.
- *Bodily-Kinesthetic intelligence* favors movement and touch to synthesize information.
- *Musical intelligence* implies musical ability or the incorporation of music and rhythm in the learning process.
- *Interpersonal intelligence* is the ability to notice and respond to the actions and attitudes of others.
- *Intrapersonal intelligence* implies a keen awareness of one's own emotions and feelings regarding the world around them.
- *Naturalist intelligence* is the ability to distinguish between ecological phenomena and utilizes the natural environment as a catalyst for learning.
- *Existential intelligence* is the awareness of and response to the fundamental questions of life.

Gardner's theories did not endorse a spiritual, religious, or intuitive intelligence. Yet his concept of existential intelligence relates to the desire to know the meaning behind our existence. For the Christian educator, that answer is undeniably spiritual. Therefore, existential intelligence can be viewed as a disposition toward spiritual quests for fundamental questions of life. Identifying activities and strategies that incorporate these intelligences makes learning more accessible for participants of all ages. We must not isolate Gardner's model to say that people only learn in one way. We can, however, incorporate Gardner's intelligences in our teaching so that every participant is reached and interactions optimize memory and sense-making.

Organizational Learning

Another learning theory that continues to be of importance was developed in 1956 by Dr. Benjamin Bloom of the University of Chicago. It is called Bloom's Taxonomy and identifies hierarchy of categories that show how learning deepens. Bloom's research suggests a progression of behaviors that explain how people recognize, process, and use information. Bloom's Taxonomy helps teachers prepare lessons that address deepening levels of understanding.

- *Knowledge* is the basic level at which individuals are able to give rote recall of facts.
- *Comprehension* is the level of understanding at which participants can explain the meaning and purpose of data and information.
- *Application* is the level where participants apply information to their situations in concrete ways.
- *Analysis* occurs when participants examine the features or parts of concepts and identify relationships among them.
- *Synthesis* is the level where participants connect information from various vantage points or sources to gain greater meaning for the concept under study.
- *Evaluation* is the highest level of understanding because learners make judgments about the purpose of the information and its use in their lives.

Bloom's Taxonomy helps Christian educators recognize whether students are actually learning. If teachers rely on the ability of students to regurgitate Bible facts as evidence of learning, students will not progress past the knowledge level and will fall short of what is needed for spiritual formation. Some learners will understand and apply the principles of faith to aspects of their lives, but transformation requires deeper application. Using Bloom's Taxonomy, teachers can encourage learners to move into the upper domains of learning (analysis, synthesis, and evaluation) where they are able to process the tenets of their faith and the circumstances of their lives. Throughout these processes, it is the Holy Spirit that helps make the transformative connections. Teachers must be sensitive to providing activities and encounters that help students reach deeper levels of understanding.

Age-Level Learning

While the theories of Gardner and Bloom address learners of all ages, Malcolm Knowles put forth a theory of adult learning known as andragogy. In contrast to pedagogy (which Knowles sees as teaching children), andragogy examines learning based on what is important to help adult learners access and utilize information. Contrasting how adults and children learn can make Knowles' ideas clear. His theory sees personal interests as the backdrop for learning encounters that adults will remember. While children rely on the teacher to direct their learning, adult learning is largely self-directed. Children and teens are compelled to go to school or to participate in learning experiences. Adults choose to participate in learning experiences. Adults make a conscious decision to have a specific experience and outcome. Children are building their knowledge base, but adults and older teens connect their learning to their life experiences. Teachers have to help children make the connections between what they are learning and its relevance to their lives. Adults, on the other hand, are able to integrate new information with their previous experiences.

Adults are goal-oriented in their learning. They tend to accept new knowledge when it demonstrates a relevant purpose. Learning for adults is self-initiated, and its effects are generally long lasting. For the Christian educator this means that relevance is the key to helping adults understand biblical content and apply it in their faith journeys. Adults seek God because they recognize their personal need for God. If teachers fail to provide opportunities for adults to connect biblical content to their lives, they miss a critical opening in the faith journey. Experience is the key for adults because they seek authentic understandings of their faith and real connections to the faith community.

Teachers should use age-appropriate strategies that open learners to spiritual encounters. Three areas of knowledge are helpful: biblical foundation, historical knowledge, and practical application. Congregational teaching begins with a biblical foundation because congregational teaching asks the question of what God would have us to know about Him and our relationship to Him. Biblical information, however, must be related to modern times. This begins when learners explore the history of the text. Asking what the people in the passage are doing or what situations provide the background of the text allows learners to see the original audience in action. There is much more to the background of any Scripture, but finding the history behind the text opens participants' understandings of how God operates in human situations. Adults need to know that God is consistent in His interactions and expectations in human life. The wise teacher uses learning theory to help students of all ages apply biblical principles to their lives.

Inductive Study and Questioning

One way to ascertain whether learners of all ages are finding the spiritual substance of the Scripture is by asking questions. This seems simple but not all questions are meaningful. Inductive study is the process of asking questions that help participants move from the general knowledge about a passage to the application of biblical concepts in their lives. Inductive questions ask students to (1) observe what the text says, (2) interpret what the text means, and then (3) apply the text to individual lives. Teachers can use these questions throughout the lesson to develop exercises that lead learners in understanding and reflection. At other times, these questions can be used as the summation or review of the lesson, which ends with application.

One idea for asking questions places them in two categories: Fat and Skinny.[107] While this sounds cute, it is very useful. Skinny questions ask learners to recall information such as a specific item or event, or to list the major points of a Bible passage. Skinny questions often begin with "who," "what," "when," and "where." The responses are usually straightforward and based on what is written in the text of the Bible, resources, or lesson material. These questions may or may not be easy. The point is that they only address the lower levels of thought. (Remember Bloom's knowledge level?) Skinny questions do not necessarily lead to application. Questions that begin with "how" or "why" require greater thought. These more robust questions ask learners to make sense of the information or to apply it in some way. They may still be "skinny," but they are beginning to address comprehension and application.

Fat questions reach a higher level of understanding. On Bloom's taxonomy, fat questions lead to analysis, synthesis, and evaluation. Fat questions ask participants to take ownership of information and concepts. For example, asking "what if" will allow learners to consider the concepts in a different light as they process the information. Fat questions ask how the Bible fits into personal lives. They allow learners to not just ask what Jesus would do; they allow them to ask what their relationship with Jesus compels them to do.

Varying the questions for review or discussion is also important. The variation of questions will trigger brain activity, memory, recall, and response. This need not be done in a strict Q and A format. Creative teachers can employ age-appropriate activities that ask the questions in various ways. When learners use art, write poems, or engage in acting out Scripture passages and application scenarios, inductive study is involved. Questioning can move class interactions from basic comprehension to analysis that identifies spiritual understanding and application.

Addressing Learners' Needs

Spirit-led teaching seeks to create an atmosphere that successfully incorporates various paths to learning. That does not mean that learning theories should be used haphazardly or that they are meant to be meshed together in a hodge-podge of activity. It is also an over-simplification to view these theories of learning as isolated methodologies. They represent general categories that can be used to develop stimuli in meeting the needs of learners. Attention span and pulsing are mentioned here as two ways to organize lesson presentations to maximize learning regardless of learners' ages. While teaching is a highly organized endeavor, it is not prescribed or formulaic. Because all learners are different, Christian educators should be aware of the special concerns that must be recognized for some learning populations.

Attention Span

Learning begins as a mental exercise. Teachers cannot impact the brain if they cannot gain learners' attention. Attention span is one's ability to concentrate. Contrary to what we think, sitting and looking attentive to the instructor is not concentrating. Long spans of reading may not help attention either. Consider how many times you have been reading and "concentrating" only to realize that you didn't remember a word you read! Prolonged activities of a single kind are generally incapable of holding our attention. When teachers allow concentrated activities such as reading and listening to dominate the learning time, they press the limits of attention.

Our memories capture best the information at the beginning and ending of a sequence. What comes between those points may not fare as well. The solution: have more start and stop points by varying activities. Adding visuals and alternating activities between age-appropriate group discussion, mini-lectures, and physical interaction helps focus attention and sustain memory. Busy work is ineffective and counterproductive. Teachers err when they string together a number of ideas that lack a cohesive purpose. Lessons and learning experiences should be presented in ways that "prime" the brain, thereby building learners' perceptions and understandings while allowing them to reflect on what they are learning.[108] Attention is greatest when instruction takes into consideration three distinct phases: time to process information, time to internally create new meaning or make sense of the information, and time to imprint the concepts."[109] When time for these phases is provided in a teaching episode, attention is increased as the brain considers these phases and engages "specialized brain activity" to accommodate learning. When that specialized activity ends, attention ends as well.[110]

Attention span can either become problematic or be used to the best advantage regardless of age. No matter how a teacher insists that children sit still, there is a limit to how long that can happen. This is more than "ants in the pants." It is how the brain is wired. A simple formula for approximating attention span in children under nine or ten years old is to identify the child's numerical age and then add two. This will give a hint about how long children can concentrate before the activity should either move to another level or be changed. For example, you can engage a five-year-old for no more than seven minutes. (For some children and activities, that will be pushing it!) Remember that this formula is only a suggestion that can give teachers an idea of how long to engage learners in concentrated activities. The situation in the classroom and a child's personal need or ability regarding the task can alter the dynamic. Use common sense and pay attention to what is going on in the session. Also, do not assume that just because adults are present in a learning situation they are paying attention. (Using the formula for adult age plus two definitely doesn't work!) Adult brains still tune in and out along the way. (How many times has someone mistakenly thought you were taking notes in a meeting at work when you were really making a grocery list?) Adults can make it "look" like they are paying attention simply because they have mastered the skill of creative distraction.

Pulsing

So how do teachers address the limits of attention span and the issue of memory? Use what some educators call "pulsing." It is the process of alternating intense activities with action-based ones. To demonstrate this, make a fist. Hold the fist as tightly as you can. Now release and relax the fingers. It takes a moment for the muscles to relax. Repeat the exercise. That is essentially how pulsing works when teaching encounters engage the brain in intense or targeted activity for a period of time and then release, essentially allowing time for the brain to process that knowledge.

In pulsed learning, varying the activities will divide the information into shorter sections. This does not mean that the teaching should be choppy. That would defeat the cohesive nature of the enterprise. Planning exactly how to pulse the information requires that each activity take attention span, memory, and reflection time into consideration. Primary-aged learners should never just be read a story. They must be asked to respond to questions as the story progresses. A change from sitting and listening to talking or moving keeps children's brains active and engaged. When children roar like a lion or walk like a king, they activate understanding and memory. With youth and adults, groups can discuss questions related to their reading and topic. In addition, discussion does not have to engage the entire class every time. Alternate the use of pairs, triads, or other small groupings so that each learner gets a chance to talk as well as listen.

Following the pulsing concept allows students to process information as they increase memory. Pulsing also gives instructors clues about what has actually been received and how to increase understanding. Adjustments can be made in the pace or content of the lesson so that learners are actually gaining from the encounter. Pulsing or interweaving activities helps achieve the goal of engaging students in an atmosphere of learning that leads to spiritual transformation.

At every age, learners have different physical, emotional, intellectual, social, and spiritual needs. We can make generalizations about people in each age category, but we can never forget that people are individuals. These teaching and learning frameworks help teachers make lessons relevant. Without variety, lessons will fail to adequately stimulate the brain and forego the opportunity to challenge every learner.

As teachers maximize attention span through the use of pulsing, they are creating a powerful environment for learning and spiritual growth.

Special Concerns

Teachers must be aware of learners with special needs as well as those individuals who struggle with traditional learning settings. The cognitive and physical challenges of some learners may be known, and churches often seek to address these needs. Churches build ramps or add elevators and lifts for people in wheelchairs or those who have other mobility issues. A screen in the sanctuary helps to insure that everyone can see what is occurring. Some churches have interpreters who use sign language or language translation to accommodate understanding. These accommodations should extend to the Christian education programs as well. For example, churches that offer sign language during the worship service should offer this same level of accommodation in Christian education.

Other learning concerns, however, may not be obvious because people in churches are often less eager to share or display their personal struggles with learning. Teachers, therefore, should be sensitive to helping everyone without embarrassing or isolating anyone. Often, simple actions create a more accessible learning environment. Using large print helps persons with vision problems. Larger print and clear design of handouts and on-screen projections keeps down frustration with learners who otherwise would strain to read a cluttered handout or see a display. Arranging seating and reducing noise levels and distractions helps with issues in hearing and creates a better learning environment.

Some issues can be addressed through types of interactions within the class. Working in groups helps those who have difficulty reading or who struggle to retain information. Rather than asking questions and then calling on specific responders, teachers should ask the question and then allow class members to volunteer to read or speak. When learner response indicates that a person did not fully understand the question or has taken the conversation in a different direction, the teacher's ability to bring the discussion back to the point without embarrassing anyone is important.

Both adults and children may exhibit behaviors in class that need to be addressed. Adult classes can usually handle a range of problems with their learners. These may include medical conditions, mental or emotional issues, or learning challenges. Children and teens, however, present a different situation. Since children are often isolated in school because of learning differences, churches should consider moving children from class to class by age rather than grade level. In some cases, moving a child to a younger or older class is necessary. This should be done without embarrassing the child. Most churches today ask parents to reveal food and other allergies, but there are examples of children whose learning needs, behavioral situations, and even physical conditions were not revealed because parents felt that God would give the teacher a solution! Whether a child or teen is showing advanced abilities, struggling with understanding, or demonstrating problems with social interactions, teachers should seek the advice of parents.

Christian education leaders must have protocols in place for helping children and teens. Every child deserves to be included in ways that respect them as learners. In a regular school setting, learning disabilities or struggles may be documented. In a Christian education setting, those same children are present but without documentation of problems. No one wants to prejudice staff against a child, but it is important for some needs to be communicated. Autism is an example of such a need. It has many levels, and addressing the concerns can be complicated. Parents of one autistic child wanted him in Sunday school but realized they had to provide a unique level of support. This was done in conjunction with counseling the parents were receiving to learn how to help their child. Each week, the father took the youngster into class and waited outside the room. He was available for help. In the meanwhile, counseling helped his son learn to interact with others. In this case, the young man was eventually able to serve as a church usher. Every case is unique, but parents and teachers must work together to help every learner see themselves and others through God's eyes. While differences in learning styles and abilities make no difference to God, they must be addressed if transformational learning is to happen.

Putting It All Together

Unfortunately, there is no one way of teaching that fits everyone. The ability to intertwine options for learning is part of the art and science of teaching. Teachers must be mindful not to over rely on the activities that apply to their own learning style. They cannot become too comfortable with presenting in only one way. They must avoid using strategies that appeal to only one learning type. If every lesson is taught in the same way, learners will soon be bored. If every lesson is presented as if each is a puzzle or a maze to be navigated, learners will be frustrated. The idea is to use variety with moderation.

Effective teaching and successful classes do not just happen. The teaching ministry is a vehicle for encouraging spiritual transformation and not just church attendance. While all teaching requires educators to know materials, technology, and resources, the Christian educator must seek the help of the Holy Spirit in creating an atmosphere for spiritual transformation. Transformation is fostered when lessons embrace the Bible, incorporate learning strategies, and provide opportunities for reflection, interaction, and participation.

It is important to design lessons that make the best use of Bible resources, teaching tools, and lesson strategies. Teaching plans should incorporate activities from the selected paths of learning to engage the brain and the spirit during the teaching encounter. The overall plan of the lesson should also focus attention on the spiritual nature of the endeavor. In order to accomplish this, CORE training must address teaching styles and lesson design.

Style, Instinct, and the Holy Spirit

A teacher's style is discerned through the balance of the art and the science of teaching. It is the way teachers present information and control the events of the learning encounter. Style conveys a teacher's confidence in knowing the material to be presented and the presentation plan that will be used. A teacher's style encompasses the techniques employed in each phase of the lesson. Style also takes into consideration the personality and passion of the teacher, as well as the authentic engagement of the class.

Teacher instinct is part of teaching style. The congregational teacher's instinct includes the ability to anticipate student behaviors and responses. It may be evident in a teacher's quick "alteration" of an activity in order to capture a teachable moment. But there is more. Teacher instinct also comprises thoughts and actions that result from one's spiritual disposition. Teacher instinct considers that the Holy Spirit is operational in a process intended to change behaviors and attitudes through spiritual encounters. The Christian educator must anticipate that the Holy Spirit will enable participants to gain knowledge, skills, attitudes, and spiritual insight through each teaching event. While the activities might be engaging and even informative, the desired spiritual transformation will not occur if the Holy Spirit is not active in the process. Even though a biblical text may be specified by curriculum, its content goes beyond the lesson at hand. A teacher's instinct is triggered by the belief that every lesson is an opportunity for learners to examine themselves as members of the body of Christ.

When teachers have not developed their own style, they tend to mimic others or go overboard with bells and whistles that lack biblical, theological, educational, and authentic content. When teachers overuse technology or overwhelm the class with piles of study guides and outlines of their presentations, they deny the artistic flow of class interactions and detract from lesson purpose. This produces classes that are staid and uninteresting despite the "show" a teacher attempts to put on. Likewise, teachers who believe that lecturing and "preaching" are the best ways to convey what learners need often miss the aim of helping participants mature as Christians. In both cases, these teachers actually put the spotlight on themselves as "experts" while removing God from the center of the room!

Lesson Design: RISE

RISE is the curriculum model developed for the CORE Training Program. It uses four facets to create Bible-centered, Spirit-led, authentic encounters in congregational settings. The process is explained in the acronym RISE:

R – Ready: Prepare for learning by identifying prior knowledge related to the general topic of study. Here, teachers trigger learners' prior experiences with either the Bible passage or the topic for discussion.

I – Ignite: Spark thinking by creatively introducing the biblical text or specific topic. Get learners excited about what specific Bible text will be examined and the outcomes that are anticipated.

S – Search: Explore the biblical text, lesson, or topic using brain-based strategies and intentional spiritual engagement. This is where the various paths to learning and application come into play. Pulsing, as well as variation, is the key to meaningful activities in this section of the lesson.

E – Extend: Provide activities that help participants continue to think about and act on new learning beyond the classroom. In Extend, teachers develop an activity that encourages personal study or reflection through outside projects, assignments, suggestions, or questions that enhance spiritual growth after class.

RISE activities lead students to acquire information, as well as spiritual insight. Appendix B provides a model of how to use RISE in a sixty-minute class where every facet of RISE incorporates the skills that are developed through the art and science of teaching.

The RISE plan welcomes the Holy Spirit and anticipates a transformative encounter. Incorporating teaching about spiritual practices or inviting students to pray to open or close class helps them grow in faith. Soliciting prayer requests and reports of answered prayer as a routine part of the class will teach learners to show care for people who are ill or in crisis. These practices should be planned as natural parts or extensions of the lesson presentation.

Many things happen in a congregational classroom, but creating classes that help learners learn must be the aim of all instruction. How teachers plan and navigate these is an indication of their style of interweaving art and science in teaching.

Helping Teachers Find their Place in the Ministry

The Orientation phase should prepare potential teachers for placement in the teaching ministry, but placement should not necessarily be automatic. The decision to place a teacher in a class should not be based solely on convenience or availability. Having children or youth in the household or even just knowing children does not mean that a person understands the behaviors, characteristics, and spiritual needs of children and youth. Some Christian education leaders have mistakenly assumed that being young is the criterion for teaching youth. By that same token, being an adult cannot be the primary criterion for teaching adults! Whether a person becomes the lead teacher, an assistant teacher, or a specialist in art, music, crafts, and other areas, placement must be approached seriously and prayerfully. The CORE model of sustainable teacher preparation identifies two approaches to determining teacher placement: inclusion and discernment.

Inclusion

Elevate the CORE proposes a sustainable program for identifying and training those in the faith community who desire to teach in order to help others in their spiritual journeys. One aim of the Orientation phase is to give potential teachers an opportunity to participate in the ministry. In CORE, this is called Inclusion. It is a formal process that provides potential teachers an opportunity to meet members of the teaching ministry, explore the administrative and communal nature of Christian education, and become familiar with the students and work of congregational teaching. This does not mean that a novice is automatically asked to teach an entire class alone. They may be partnered with an experienced teacher and, if appropriate, allowed to share a small part in the lesson presentation. They may also assist with secretarial or administrative duties or monitor and help children or teens. In this way, Inclusion allows potential teachers and ministry leaders the freedom to decide whether a Christian education assignment is appropriate.

Discernment

Discernment is the process of seeking divine guidance in order to make a decision or a judgment. Ministry leaders have a responsibility to help potential teachers discern their place in the ministry. It has already been established that the teacher's knowledge of the Bible and God are the key starting points. Additionally, leaders must be willing to discuss how assignments were completed and what insights were gained. Leaders must carefully observe classes and determine if potential teachers understand the learners and strategies. They must take into consideration teachers' attitudes and dispositions. It is also important to encourage individuals to determine if their responsibilities and lifestyles will allow them time to commit to the teaching assignment and the ministry. A spiritual gifts survey should have been administered as part of Call. If it wasn't administered earlier, it should be completed before placement is made. There is always work to be done in Christian education and in addition to teaching, there are many roles to fill. Individual teachers should reflect on their surveys and leaders can help them match their profiles to specific areas of work and ministry. Prayerful consideration of these matters will help church leaders and potential teachers identify appropriate areas based on the individual's gift, talent, skill, and call.

Placement

Regardless of how and when a church places teachers in an assignment, the decision should be made prayerfully. In some churches and denominations, a teaching assignment is essentially permanent. In other congregations, assignments are for specific periods of time such as Vacation Bible School or some special adult or teen series of classes.

The CORE approach should not be abandoned because short-term assignments are needed. CORE seeks to prepare Christian educators before they are needed.

Placing a teacher in the wrong area can create stress for the teacher and the learners. Placing someone in a situation without giving them ample support and assistance can be devastating and deter them from participation in the ministry all together. Deciding on placement may mean getting additional insight to help make the choice. In children's programs, placement of teachers and workers requires screening through appropriate legal channels. Background checks should be mandatory for workers in this area. These can be arranged through independent agencies or the church's insurance company. While the involvement of the pastor in the Christian education ministry may vary, a wise Christian education leader will discuss potential teachers with the pastor. The pastor's insight is broad and includes the theology and ideology regarding the direction of Christian education. The pastor may also know more about the person or be more sensitive to circumstances and experiences in the person's life than anyone else in the church. In churches that have Christian education boards or teams, the input and consensus of those members must be considered also.

In some cases, a person in Orientation may decide not to enter a formal teaching assignment right away. Later something may occur that makes the potential teacher "ready and able" to begin Christian education work. Some may decide to be involved intermittently or for special assignments only. In other cases the potential teacher may identify an assignment in a ministry outside of teaching. Whatever the outcome, not taking an assignment is neither a failure nor a setback because everything learned in Call and Orientation is valuable to members of the faith community.

Summary

Orientation is the introduction to teaching. Although churches may choose to offer their initial Orientation classes to current teachers, as CORE continues, classes should be provided before teachers embark on their assignments in Christian education. Orientation sessions help teachers expand their knowledge regarding nurturing the spiritual transformation of learners. They provide the opportunity for potential and current teachers to explore and use the resources and tools that enhance learner knowledge. Instruction in Orientation helps teachers recognize and practice skills that deepen their understanding of how student learning is enhanced through their knowledge of brain-based strategies and their understanding of learner needs.

When congregational teachers accrue personal libraries of resources that include a variety of Bibles, biblical references, and educational resources, they are learning to apply the science of teaching and learning in Bible-centered and Spirit-led encounters. Teachers who complete Orientation should be able to develop meaningful learning experiences that open the door to the work of the Holy Spirit. This doesn't happen all at once. Learning to teach is a process and, with time, those who are called to teach get better at doing it.

Persons who engage in the Orientation process will experience a spiritual journey where the work of the ministry of teaching is front and center. When Orientation is completed, Christian education leaders, new and continuing teachers, and the congregation at large are able to celebrate these individuals and the teaching ministry as the Holy Spirit enhances learners' lives and congregational goals are met.

Consider:

1. Assess your personal library. What resources do you need to fill your "gaps?"
2. Use the RISE model to prepare a demonstration of a favorite resource. Share your demonstration with others.
3. Analyze your learning style according to Gardner's Theory of Multiple Intelligences. How does that compare to how you teach?
4. Write a summary of each of these instructional factors:

a. Pulsing

b. Questioning

c. Attention span

d. Memory

e. Brain-based strategies

5. How might you apply the principles of andragogy to older youth or young adults?

6. Explain the benefits of Inclusion and how you would enhance it.

CHAPTER ELEVEN

R – Refining:
Furthering Knowledge and Skill

Next Steps

President Harry S. Truman is reported to have said, "It's what you learn after you know it all that counts." There is no single class or experience that can prepare congregational teachers for everything they will encounter. Even experienced teachers need to sharpen their skills periodically. Teachers are not exempt from lifelong learning regardless of how gifted and heralded their teaching may be. Paul's admonition to Timothy to "stir up the gift" can well be applied to teaching (2 Timothy 1:6).

Once they have started teaching, instructors will have questions. "Why did I have trouble with this strategy?" "How do I get the group on track after we've been taken off course?" "I am doing all the right things in class, but *my* devotional life is slipping. What can I do?" When teachers are reflective of their call, they strive to create meaningful learning experiences for students. Sessions in the Refining process build on Orientation to help teachers seamlessly intertwine teaching skill with artistic passion. Refining helps teachers grapple with teaching styles, addressing learners' needs, and identifying ways to be more intentional about guiding students in their spiritual quests.

Options for Refining Sessions

This chapter offers five options to support teacher learning during the Refining phase: **Lifeline Cohorts, Coaching, Enhancement Seminars, Community Learning Opportunities,** and **Focused Meetings**. The launch of the Refining phase of CORE will vary with congregational needs, church and participant calendars, church and personal finances, and space. One church may decide to only offer one Refining activity each year. Another may offer all five options and allow teachers to individually select which seems most fitting for them. No one is expected to participate in all five options in a single year. Some participants may never take all five options. Whether a church starts new teachers in short-term Lifeline Cohorts or only offers Enhancement Seminars and Community Learning periodically, it is important that Refining happens.

The Refining process cannot be neglected. In order to elevate the level of teaching in the local congregation, teacher knowledge must be respected as a core tenet of the endeavor. If Refining is treated as an unnecessary "extra," the level of engagement in congregational classes will decrease, and new opportunities to enhance spiritual development will be missed.

Lifeline Cohorts

On a popular TV game show, contestants were given the opportunity to answer questions for cash prizes. If a question was too difficult, contestants had the option of using their "lifeline" to call a friend for help. That strategy has merit. When new teachers receive ministry assignments, they benefit from placement in a Lifeline Cohort, a small group of teachers who gather periodically on a short-term basis to share their concerns. Proverbs 11:14 says that "in the multitude of counsellors there is safety." Lifeline Cohorts serve as accountability partners, teaching friends, and prayer partners who support one another as co-laborers seeking to serve the body of Christ through teaching.

The size and makeup of Lifeline Cohorts can vary. While group members may or may not be novices, at least one of the partners should be an experienced congregational teacher who can serve as the convener. Even though the more experienced person may encourage the conversation, that person is not "in charge." It is important not to imply a hierarchy where any person or sub-group has greater power than others in the group. The diversity of these groups assures different perspectives. Their conversations can lead to new teaching ideas and give members the courage to try them.

The initial Lifeline Cohort meeting must be face-to-face. The cohort can be a very useful tool as teachers enter the ministry or start new ministry assignments. Groups might decide to meet weekly or monthly. Gathering times should be short, possibly one hour, either on the telephone, in person, or online. During the meetings, the convener should see to it that everyone who wants to speak at a session has the opportunity to do so. Periodically, an entire session may be devoted to one or two teacher's concerns. When these sessions occur, members should focus on listening and helping one another think through problems. No one can demand that their views be accepted. Of course, family matters, work-related issues, gossip, and personal gripes have no place in Lifeline discussions.

It is important, too, that all groups have established boundaries. Time boundaries must be negotiated so that meetings do not become burdensome. Once decided upon, time limits and meeting times should be maintained. Any change in time must be agreed upon by the *entire* cohort. Confidentiality must be maintained as well. For example, when individuals provide contact information, members must agree not to share the information with people outside the Lifeline Cohort. Above all, members must be mentally and physically present in the conversation. Whether groups meet on the telephone, online, or in person, members should avoid texting, checking emails, and making or receiving calls. Such actions are rude and distracting, sending a message of disinterest in the work and the teaching partners.

Leaders always have the option of joining a Lifeline Cohort in order to ascertain that groups are functioning as they should. But caution should be taken to avoid disrupting the group dynamic. A leader's involvement in the Lifeline Cohort is an opportunity to give and get fresh ideas or make suggestions regarding problems and issues teachers are facing.

Coaching

Coaching can be defined as a process used to guide someone in enhancing or improving a skill. It is used in education as well as business, sports, and other fields to aid performance. Exodus 18:13–26 and Matthew 14:15–21 provide biblical examples of coaching. In the Exodus account, Jethro has a conversation with his son-in-law, Moses. The older man observes Moses at work and identifies the issues he sees as needing improvement. Jethro then explains a plan that would yield better outcomes. In Matthew, Jesus coaches the disciples by instructing them to feed the 5000-plus gathered onlookers. Jesus poses a question, allows the disciples to respond, develops a teaching assignment, and guides their actions in a way that lets them "test" their knowledge.

As part of the Refining process, coaching may either be offered as a choice for interested teachers, an opportunity that can be requested by a teacher, or an option provided by a ministry leader who is aware of what a teacher needs. Regardless of how the coaching situation is initiated, coaches work alongside teachers, guiding them so that they can operate independently with better results.

Coaching generally partners an experienced teacher with a novice, or a person who has specific insight with a person who can benefit from that assistance. The coach does not have to be the ministry leader. Neither can the choice of a coach be based on longevity. Coaching selections should consider personality, gender, and the age level taught. Effective teaching, as well as the coach's expertise in the needed area, must be considered as well. When coaching assignments are made, the parties should agree on the ground rules and boundaries regarding how the coaching will be undertaken.

In the CORE Refining process, coaching is a short-term, one-on-one opportunity for teachers to discuss their teaching issues and seek help. While the coaching arrangement may only last a few weeks, there may be occasions when a coach might be assigned to a specific teacher for a longer period. The coaching process largely consists of observation and listening. It is not the setting for "fixing" the teacher's problems. It is the place for questions and discussions that either lead the teacher to a solution, a consideration of an alternate action, or a determination to hone skills. When the experience is completed, the coach helps the teacher debrief the process and outcomes. When coaching is done respectfully and in a focused manner, it will encourage the faith journeys of both individuals.

Enhancement Seminars

CORE Enhancement Seminars are general gatherings around a single topic or issue that is of value to at least one segment of the Christian Education Department. Churches have long offered classes or seminars that fall into this category. Unfortunately, they often serve as the only preparation teachers received. Such disjointed seminars seem to borrow from Jesus' parable in Mark 4: some instructional seeds fall by the wayside and others fall on stony ground where they cannot take root. Instead, CORE Enhancement Seminars build upon what teachers have learned and experienced in the Call and Orientation segments, creating a more substantive approach to ongoing learning.

These seminar-like gatherings may be conducted for one hour or more, either as single sessions or a series. For example, a single session could focus on developing creative questions or helping learners tell their faith stories. A series of Enhancement Seminars on puppetry would appeal to those who teach children, but each session would focus on one specific aspect of puppetry such as how to help children make sock puppets.

Whether Enhancement Seminars are led by Christian education ministry leaders, selected clergy, or other knowledgeable members of the congregation, they provide periodic opportunities for refining teacher knowledge and skills. They offer time to share, brainstorm, or reflect on issues and topics that are germane to groups of teachers.

Community Learning Opportunities

Community Learning Opportunities offer single learning options that engage Christian educators in outside events. Although they occur as regular activities outside the church, these events can be used as Refining sessions in the CORE process. This can include a variety of community events such as plays or museum outings that may be theologically or biblically instructive. A gathering that involves a community event does not require a Bible-related topic. Churches should consider these gatherings for teachers and staff, but might also want to include them as opportunities for students and teachers to have a fun experience as they learn to share as members of God's family.

Focused Meetings

Because these sessions have been a "misplaced" staple in Christian education programs, their content and format is quite familiar. Enhancement Seminars can be general or targeted for teachers who share a specific age group or program such as Vacation Bible School. These training experiences increase the likelihood of teachers networking with and learning from others.

Refinement sessions that take the form of regularly scheduled gatherings connect teachers to ministry life. Some Christian education departments meet weekly or monthly. When meetings are held frequently, they generally last one hour. The "teachers meeting" concept is based on a format that has provided decades of Christian education training. It remains a staple in some denominations. While some churches have abandoned the practice, others continue to see merit in regularly touching bases with those in the ministry. Originally, these sessions were designed to help Sunday school teachers prepare for weekly instruction. Many churches have adopted an online version of these regularly scheduled options to accommodate hectic schedules.

The real benefit of regularly scheduled meetings comes from the power of this traditional format to provide opportunities for teachers to collectively gain understanding of a biblical passage or teaching unit. This format also allows time for teachers to demonstrate how they plan to teach a given lesson. Since involvement in the life of the church is critical to faith development, regularly scheduled meetings provide an opportunity for teachers to plan communal activities for themselves or their collective classes.

Quarterly or biannual sessions allow churches to provide two- to three-hour training events. This format can offer a variety of topics or provide time for reflection, questions, and networking within the mini-conference format. An annual conference can partner two or more churches who could then offer several sessions in a single day and broaden teachers' networking base.

The Content of Refining Options

Content for Refining sessions is meant to enrich the knowledge, skills, and behaviors developed during and since Orientation. The Refining process creates multiple opportunities for teachers to reflect on their attitudes and spiritual dispositions, especially regarding teaching the Bible and its applications. The options are totally determined by the local church, but the content of these sessions should focus on three areas: teaching skill, Bible knowledge, and faith development. By addressing these areas, Refining provides an opportunity to revisit or refocus what was learned in both Call and Orientation.

Refining Teaching Skills

Teaching skills can always be sharpened and expanded. While teachers received an overview of teaching during Orientation, the Refining phase seeks to deepen or solidify their understanding of instructional areas. Refining sessions can provide opportunities for teachers to engage in hands-on training or learn more about materials and strategies for specific age groups.

Refining options can take any format. Teachers might discuss books, Internet articles, or other periodicals on specific skills or age-level concerns in workshops, meetings, small group gatherings or online discussion groups. Experienced teachers usually enjoy sharing their knowledge with others, making it possible for any church to create

Refining events using the talent available in the church or community. Events hosted by publishing houses and denominations provide opportunities to network and learn. Many educational organizations, colleges, and online teaching groups post videos and host webinars that can help with teaching skills. Topics might include the following:

- building a personal library of teaching or Bible study resources;
- using lexicons and concordances to improve Bible knowledge;
- enhancing memory, increasing attention, or using learning games;
- learning more about creating questions that help learners apply biblical knowledge; and
- addressing learning styles.

Refining Bible Knowledge

Meaningful congregational teaching hinges on the teachers' comprehension of biblical texts. The Refining stage seeks to help teachers expand that knowledge. Here, teachers might take a theological or historical dive into the Bible. Refining sessions can focus on equipping teachers with additional strategies to conduct inductive Bible studies or deepen teachers' knowledge of systematic theology and doctrinal tenets that undergird their faith. Refining opportunities that utilize books, videos, or websites will be helpful. Often, a simple Internet search can yield helpful information on Bible history or culture. Community organizations such as museums often present exhibits, symposia, or talks on topics related to the Bible, Bible lands, archaeology, or historic eras or people that can enhance Bible background.

Refining Faith

The faith of teachers is critical to anything they do in the teaching ministry. Congregational teaching helps learners and teachers navigate the spiritual terrain of the Christian journey. Refining sessions can provide opportunities for teachers to learn more about their personal application of spiritual disciplines and re-examine their own relationship with Jesus Christ. As part of the Refining process, teachers might attend a retreat or participate in a special worship service, Bible conference, or denomination convention. Teachers may form book clubs to read non-fiction or inspirational materials that strengthen their faith. Refining sessions can bring new energy to a teacher's personal study and preparation while providing a safe space for teachers to reflect on the specifics of their spiritual journeys.

Making Refining Options Happen

Refining sessions can focus on increasing knowledge and augmenting skills, but remember that developing relationships among teachers and learners can open the door to developing Christian attitudes and spiritual dispositions. Not every church has the capacity to provide Refining options independently. When local churches pool resources, getting quality training for teacher candidates and current teachers becomes more attainable. Sharing expenses means that each church benefits, costs are lessened, and churches have new options for learning, networking, and fellowship. Before creating any opportunity, make sure the purpose is clear and that guidelines have been established.

Take Advantage of Free Events

Free community concerts, sporting events, cultural experiences, or educational gatherings make excellent outings. Many of these ventures require tickets or registration, even if they are free. Leaders should set clear deadlines and publicize the event well in advance. If necessary, identify a time to cancel the venture if the response is too low. Sometimes, especially when tickets are free, people fail to show up and cause others to not have a seat because the venue thought they were full.

Plan for Events that Cost

Community Learning Opportunities may seem endless, but they need careful planning. There are obviously many events that cost money and have great appeal for a shared outing. Theatrical and sporting events, opportunities to hear speakers or artists, or attending movies that are cultural blockbusters fall in this category. These events can lead to meaningful discussions that reflect on matters of faith and life. It is important to prepare participants about what to expect and what they will gain; it is a learning experience. Even if it just seems like a fun outing, expect teachable moments to arise. When your intent is clear from the beginning, you can better plan and debrief the activity.

Know the Financial and Legal Obligations

There are a few things to consider when arranging a Community Learning Opportunity. Many times, teachers who are friends agree upon a venture only to discover that the pastor has an issue, the funds are not available, or the church schedule conflicts with their plans. Before venturing out, "consider the cost." Failing to do so could damage future chances for hosting such events. Here are a few tips:

- Get an exact understanding of the costs and resources. If you are partnering with another church or group to make the opportunity available, be clear about what the shared responsibilities will be. An estimate will not do and may cause irreparable damage when one of the partners feels abused by the situation. Many an idea has seemed simple but turned into a nightmare of embarrassment, confusion, and frustration due to poor planning.
- Before engaging in any event—regardless of whether it calls for a written contract (but especially if it does)—make sure approval has been given. Begin with getting approval by the pastor, trustees, or other church leaders who are authorized to make decisions of this type. Persons at the highest level of leadership in both the local church and the partner facility should have the responsibility of signing off on the venture. If the pastor or ministry leader does not attend the event, make sure to report the outcome as both a courtesy and a way of being accountable.
- Make sure all legal issues are addressed. If any children or youth

are attending, make sure the adults who interact with them have completed the background checks and the students have signed permission slips. (It is a good idea to leave a copy of those slips with the church and to take a copy with you in case of emergencies.) Remember that renting a bus or driving individual cars can present issues of liability. Again, make sure that the proper leadership has given consent.

Summary

Teaching is more than just transmitting content. Congregational teachers need to have their skills sharpened, their artistic senses heightened, and their spiritual lives nourished. Teachers in the Refining process need opportunities to reflect on their teaching, Bible knowledge, and faith journeys. They also need opportunities to use and hone their skills and abilities as congregational teachers. Refining classes may be taken as cohort sessions with all participating teachers in each class offered. However, if possible, there may be times when teachers can self-select the Refining activities that are most helpful to them. On occasion, Refining options can also be offered to students and other congregants. It is important to remember that the Refining stage includes targeted learning and expanded activities that enhance ministry skills and purpose.

Consider

1. Compare the benefits of Lifeline Cohorts, Coaching, Enhancement Seminars, Community Learning Opportunities, and Focused Meetings. How does each contribute to the instructional and spiritual development of teachers? Which of the formats in Refining do you think is of the greatest benefit?
2. This chapter identifies three Refining focus areas—teaching, Bible knowledge, and faith. Why are these critical? Is there any other area you would include? Why?

3. Several suggestions for scheduling Refining sessions are presented in this chapter. Is there a different format that you would add?

4. Several Community Learning Opportunities are listed in this chapter. What additional options can you envision?

5. If you were to train the coaches for the Coaching phase, what would you consider to be the most important skills they should develop?

6. Several legal considerations were identified in this chapter. They are important to creating a successful community event but just a few examples to consider. Can you add anything to the list?

CHAPTER TWELVE

E – Enrichment: Strengthening the Ministry

Developing Leaders

When Jesus called the first of His disciples, He simply said, "Follow me and I will make you fishers of men" (Matthew 4:19). The Twelve became a cohort dedicated to Jesus and His vision. In the next three years, they were led to new understandings. Peter's response to Jesus' question of "Who do men say that I am?" was the proof his basic knowledge of the God of Israel had changed (Matthew 16:13–17). For those three years, Jesus presented a new orientation to what it meant to serve others. When the disciples were coached and sent out two-by-two, they returned with a new revelation of what could be done in ministry (Mark 6:7–13, 30). On the day of Pentecost, when Peter rose to preach the message of the Good News, the disciples had become leaders able to contribute to the transformation of those around them (Acts 3).

CORE creates or identifies learning opportunities that strengthen the life of the congregation, enhance the essential features of teaching, and allow teachers to expand their capacity to teach. At this point in other Christian Education training programs, the final step would be maintenance: maintaining skills and maintaining involvement. Throughout the CORE process, participants' actions of faith, as well as their attitudes and spiritual dispositions, have been enhanced. Their knowledge, skills, and teaching behaviors have been sharpened.

When congregational teachers reach the Enrichment phase, they are often amazed at what they actually know about teaching, their students, the Bible, and themselves. Because the process of CORE training has followed the model set forth by Jesus for service or ministry in the church teachers are prepared to be servant-leaders. This does not negate the service they have already provided. Neither does it make the assumption that all teachers aspire to be in positions of power in local assemblies. CORE Enrichment is based on the idea that as each person grows in faith and service they will desire to contribute more to the work of the Kingdom. As John Maxwell put it, "A leader is one who knows the way, goes the way, and shows the way."[111] By the time they reach Enrichment, teachers will have followed their path to leadership and service.

The CORE Learning Plan

Teachers in the Enrichment process are invited to share their learning goals in a CORE Learning Plan. The plan can be part of an annual review or, if teachers have short-term assignments, it can be useful at the beginning of the assignment and as a culminating review of their service. The Learning Plan format can be as simple as a form, a notebook, or a computer file where teachers express what they have observed and done, as well as what they want to learn and do as part of the ministry. CORE Learning Plans are shared with ministry leaders who are responsible for giving teachers guidance. Enrichment asks teachers to develop an annual goal or goals they believe will help them in the Christian Education Department. For some people, the goal might be to attend a symposium or conference. For others it could include a workshop or an encounter related to their career choices. The object is to identify an action that can enrich their learning and subsequently their teaching. Because of this, the goal can range from decluttering workspace at home, to reading a book by a noted educator or seeking out a personal teaching mentor.

Managing the CORE Learning Plan Process

While identifying a personal goal for the CORE Learning Plan may be a personal decision, it is neither a secret effort nor done in isolation. Each year, ministry leaders should schedule time to discuss goals, progress, and concerns with individual teachers. This leads to better support and fresh direction for the ministry. This need not be a complicated process, but it does require ministry leaders and teachers to talk formally about what teachers are doing to grow in the ministry. When teachers' self-identified enrichment option(s) are placed on their learning plans, the teacher and the ministry are aware of how teachers think about their own learning and ministry work.

During Enrichment, CORE Learning Plan conversations with teachers should be formal without being intimidating. This is not an interrogation; it is a conversation about congregational teaching and the well-being of Christian educators and those they teach. The formality of the conversation comes in finding a time when the leader and the teacher are available for discussion and setting parameters for the talk. Generally, a half hour is sufficient. Teachers should also know why the talk is scheduled. Whether Christian educators are asked to bring a formal plan with them or provide a plan as follow-up to the conversation is a matter of style. However, having a format for thinking about and presenting their options allows teachers to give critical consideration to what they will do to enhance their teaching and learning options.

Keep the Learning Plan questions short and sweet. The object is to start a discussion, not turn off helpers. The conversation should address the current status of the teachers' work and their efforts to hone their skills and refine their efforts to encourage the faith journey of congregants. These conversations should also include discussion about any challenges teachers are facing and any support that they feel is needed in order for them to be the teachers and servant-leaders they have been called to be. Without prying, ministry leaders must also let teachers talk about their families, careers, and other obligations. A learning plan can only be developed in the context of teachers' lived experiences. When teachers are raising children, caring for ill relatives, or facing health challenges, ministry leaders must recognize their personal situations. Ministry leaders should be aware of and committed to supporting teachers in prayer and with other assistance as needed.

The CORE Learning Plan and Accountability

The CORE Learning Plan is a critical piece of the sustainable teacher training process. It provides an avenue of accountability and transparency for teachers and leaders. The plan can actually be introduced in both Orientation and Refinement because it helps facilitate needed conversation in Christian education. Too often, ministry leaders leave teachers, especially veteran teachers, on their own without ever taking the temperature of the department or class. Doing that leaves teachers to develop isolated relationships with their classes. Loyalties to the teacher or the class can develop without any consideration of their affiliation with the church. In some cases, ministry leaders have been shocked to learn that teachers have strayed from the prescribed course or are teaching a theological or doctrinal stance that is contradictory to the faith tradition. When such silos of relationships are developed, new comers are discouraged, the faith tradition is undermined, and cliques rather than vibrant classes are created. Needless to say, ministry leaders should always be observant of what classes and teachers are doing in order to avoid complacency and honor the voices and experiences of teachers and students.

As teachers develop their CORE Learning Plans, they should be encouraged to independently seek out and attend seminars, workshops, retreats, online/virtual learning experiences, or other activities that can enrich them as leaders and teachers. When teachers are driven by their awareness to their call, they will develop fresh perspectives that can breathe new life into classes, teacher interactions, and other areas of the church's ministry. As a result of their CORE learning experiences, teachers are able to share their suggestions about ways to improve the ministry.

Identifying Enrichment and Leadership Options

Teachers in the Enrichment phase of CORE should be given flexibility in identifying and even designing their own leadership involvement. Ministry leaders should avoid the temptation to assign leadership responsibilities based on their needs rather than teacher readiness for leadership responsibilities. Likewise, not giving teachers who undertake new roles the support they need is discouraging. The keys to enrichment are balance and respect. Teaching should not become overwhelming or burdensome. It is definitely a commitment, but it should not become a problem that teachers cannot commit to! The leadership aspect of Enrichment is a natural next step. Leadership need not be labeled as such, but it is the recognition that teachers are engaged in helping other teachers, as well as students, in enhanced ways.

Self-Directed Options

Whatever teachers and leaders determine to be the best enrichment options should take into consideration how these activities— whether they have a natural religious orientation or not— can be related to faith and learning. Teachers' independent learning options result in metacognition, the ability to consciously observe how one learns. No matter the content, teachers may be discovering their own learning styles, which will make them more keenly aware of how students learn. They will likely be involved in ventures that use technology in ways they may not have considered before. This will increase their interest in the importance of technology, visuals, and audio options in their own instructional plans.

Even though teachers may be identifying and exercising new skills, they still need guidance and coaching to develop fully. Ministry leaders should be prepared to help some individuals identify what they can do to enhance their learning based on their real lives. The object is not to stress teachers but to help them see lifelong learning as part of their life journey. For example, a teacher who states she will take a college course is not likely to achieve that goal if she has three children and works a full-time job—unless that course is mandated by the workplace or another activity already in progress. This is based on the "so-many-hours-in-a-day" rule. Some individuals may have the support they need to alter their schedules to take a course, but others will find it difficult to juggle. These are the teachers who will be discouraged and feel overwhelmed. When that happens, these are the teachers who are most likely to leave the Christian education ministry—either for a time or permanently. Consider, however, that the same teacher is coaching a scout troop. Learning opportunities related to scouting could become part of the goal. Whether the learning is tangential to teaching or mandated by another activity in their lives, the ministry leader needs to help teachers see where the activities enrich their learning and can be adapted to enhance learning in a congregational setting.

When Christian educators are engaged in self-directed learning, they should be invited to make presentations highlighting what they have learned and how it relates to their faith walk and their Christian education involvement. When teachers identify a self-directed opportunity that reaches the desired goal of their learning plan, they should be encouraged to pursue it. The overall effect: Congregational teachers will become better teachers and take the lead in helping others learn.

Leadership Opportunities in Christian Education

The Enrichment phase should also provide teachers with leadership opportunities. For example, teachers can serve as conveners in Lifeline Cohorts. Inviting teachers to model specific skills or demonstrate a technique or strategy they have used in their classes gives opportunities for leadership as teachers step into the "trainer" role to share their ideas with others. Allow potential and new teachers to shadow those who have completed CORE. This enhances leadership skills and encourages new individuals to teach.

Teachers in Enrichment may enjoy being coaches to new teachers or those who can benefit from their experience or expertise. Coaching not only improves ability, but it also increases leadership skills, sharpens communication, and engenders faith in God. The congregational teacher who seeks or is assigned to a coaching situation may be a person who is beginning or already committed to a ministry position. Let's say a teacher who desires to communicate better with the parents of youth requests a coach to help in that area. The coach would sit with the teacher, listen to the issues at hand, and determine what specific help the teacher wants or needs. The two would then identify a time and place when the coach could observe the teacher's communication style. After observation, the coach may suggest ideas such as a parent coffee chat, an open house, and or a monthly newsletter that the teachers and learners create together. The coach might also give guidance for how the teacher can follow through on the project.

Selecting the coach should be done carefully. Unless a coach has amazing skill and a diverse background, a person who teaches preschoolers will probably not make a good coach for someone who teaches adults. Gender may also need to be taken into consideration. If the teacher asking to have a coach is a man who teaches ten-year-old boys, a woman is well able to serve as coach. On the other hand, a man may be able to step in to observe without altering the dynamic in the room. In other cases, gender difference can create unexpected personal problems. For example, some spouses are uncomfortable with telephone calls or meetings that they feel are infringing on personal time and space. To avoid these and other problems, the coach and the teacher must have ground rules that respect personal space and time.

Leadership can also be developed through writing. This can include inviting teachers who have abilities in communication skills to write articles for the church bulletin, community paper, or denominational magazine. Articles might provide information on the essential features of Christian education, explain Bible passages, or highlight what is happening in the Christian education program at your church. Curriculum writing is another leadership area. Providing opportunities that encourage teachers to develop curricula can lead to new classes and renewed thinking about what teachers do in classes and learning encounters. The writing aspect can also be achieved as teachers with skills in web design and marketing use their knowledge to promote

Christian education to the larger church community or beyond the church walls.

Other avenues for leadership opportunities are available through denominational, community, or global ministries. Involvement in Christian education at these levels extends teacher knowledge vastly. Through these venues, teachers are able to meet new people with whom they share common interests and gifts. Their own vision for ministry is heightened as they appreciate the contributions of others. Periodic opportunities to work with denominational and community groups that reach out to local residents can be exciting reminders of the aim of the Gospel. Engaging in global ministry expands and clarifies the scope of ministry work as teachers realize their potential as teacher-leaders.

Summary

As in Refinement, teachers in Enrichment are encouraged to determine self-identified options that help them exercise leadership. Congregational and ministry leaders can be the conduit for identifying community experiences and classes to suggest to teachers. For example, teachers who are serious about knowing the Bible will often seek several avenues of learning on their own. These may include events such as conferences, workshops, or retreats offered by other churches or groups. But ministry leaders should always be creative in helping teachers stretch their skills and vision to reach their goals in Christian education and life. The ideas below summarize the Enrichment options mentioned in this chapter that help churches develop dynamic teachers, leaders, and educational ministries.

1. Give teachers opportunities to create projects, programs, and new classes.
2. Train experienced teachers to convene Lifeline Cohorts or to be coaches in the Refining phase.
3. Have new and potential teachers shadow more experienced teachers.
4. Teachers in Enrichment might become coaches for other teachers.

5. Identify opportunities for teachers to contribute to denominational, community, or global work.

Consider

1. What further suggestions can you make for Enrichment activities in leadership development or creating self-directed options?
2. What would you expect the spiritual lives of teachers at the Enrichment level to be? Why?
3. Leadership may not mean that every teacher will step to the front of the line. For some teachers, leadership means gaining confidence to operate effectively in teaching. How would you determine the type and level of leadership teachers were exhibiting?
4. Do you agree that leadership is a natural progression for teacher development? Why?
5. Design a CORE Learning Plan that can be used in your church to help teachers reflect on their learning and leadership.
6. Complete your personal Core Learning Plan. What does it reveal about you?

Realizing the Power
of an Elevated CORE

Moving Forward

Teaching that is Bible-centered, life-focused, and spirit-led is more than just effective teaching. It is teaching that supports God's desire for His Spirit to dwell in the hearts of people. The learners' faith is critical to receiving the Word of God. The transformative and transcendent nature of the Bible and Bible study will change hearts and lives. God does the transformative work, but "God uses teaching to bring faith to life."[112]

Jesus Christ, who is "the same yesterday, and to day, and for ever," is never without a witness (Hebrews 13:8). No generation is ever bereft of God's love or grace. Yet, today we are increasingly aware of the differences between a generation that questions the traditions of faith practiced by their parents and grandparents and the generations that held those traditions often without question. Because its roots are in the nineteenth century, some have argued that the Christian education movement is outdated, still trapped in its history of Sunday school and children's programs. Others have abandoned any robust effort to include non-clergy as viable teachers of the Gospel, claiming that such teaching is automatically shallow. Some people believe that the only way for a church to be effective is if it is driven by a mega-sense of worship and the name recognition of a charismatic pastor or global leader. As a result, too many Christian education programs have been rendered ineffective and isolated from the lives of those they wish to help. There must be common ground—and Elevate the CORE has advocated for such an approach.

A Case Study

The CORE model grew out of work that was started at the Apostolic Church of God in Chicago in 2004. At that point, the over seventy-year-old church had more than twenty thousand members. Located in the heart of the Woodlawn community on Chicago's south side, Apostolic Church of God was both progressive and traditional in its internal and outreach programs. For example, the church still hosted the robust Sunday Morning Bible Study (SMBS) program with over one thousand members who met at 8:00 A.M. each week. The pastor, Bishop Arthur M. Brazier, was a community activist, a civil rights leader, and a faithful pastor who cared deeply about the economically and socially diverse congregation. Because Bishop Brazier believed fully in the preparation of non-clergy and clergy for the work of the ministry, he eagerly supported all elements of the church's teaching ministry.

In the meanwhile, the SMBS director was seeking God about how to develop a program that took teachers from the basics of Bible instruction to new levels of action and energy in its offerings.[113] In an effort to reorganize the training program, the director identified four areas and proceeded to flesh out what a new program would entail. Based on its traditional programs, the church had already incorporated facets of "Call" in its classes for new members, plus SMBS included elements of Call in a few of its elective classes. Teachers had always been encouraged to attend special training opportunities offered by various para-church organizations and segments of their denomination—local, statewide and national—but only about one-fourth of the teachers engaged in those workshops and seminars. Segments of the teaching population were moving forward but others were not as engaged in increasing their skills as Christian educators.

The SMBS initial teacher training (Orientation) program was strong and had been in place for over fifteen years. The problem was that attempts at additional training often seemed haphazard and unproductive. It was clear to Christian education leadership that a different level of ongoing training was necessary if they were to address the needs of an expanding congregation and a developing teaching staff that now incorporated multiple generations of teachers. Many members of the church had taken classes at local seminaries and Bible colleges. Several Sunday Christian education leaders identified a program taught at Moody Bible Institute they felt could help address the emerging Christian education issues because they fit the vision and mission of a redesigned training program for the Apostolic Church of God. After discussion, the pastor and leadership team for Sunday Morning Bible Study saw merit in developing cohorts to take those external classes.

Dr. Dale Johnson offered comprehensive three-tiered continuing education course at Moody. It was decided that his course offerings would become the "next level" of training (Refinement) for Christian educators in the Apostolic Church of God Sunday Morning Bible Study program. Dr. Johnson was asked to teach the courses at the church. They would be the same courses taught at Moody for the same credit; only the location would change. Bishop Brazier supported the effort and eagerly authorized SMBS ministry funds to be used to register its teachers as continuing education students at Moody. Initially, twenty experienced teachers self-selected enrollment in the weekly Moody classes, which were taught on Saturdays. Teaching skills and Bible knowledge were developed through in-class and external assignments.

As the courses progressed, new cohorts were added with those classes being taught on week nights. New cohort members included individuals who taught in various children and teen ministries at the Apostolic Church of God. While the church did not pay for the new cohorts, individuals determined that the effort was worth the investment. Many of the clergy and congregation members who taught in prison and community outreach programs took advantage of this opportunity to learn. Individuals from other churches requested to be included. Eventually, other churches also recognized the value of this process and offered classes to their congregations.

Dr. Johnson's classes were rigorous and raised the level of knowledge, skills, behaviors, attitudes, and spiritual dispositions of each person. Teachers' learning soared as they discovered new perspectives on the role of congregational teaching. All of these teachers, many of whom had taught over a decade, were secure in their personal faith journeys, but some had grown stagnant in identifying ways to help the changing church population grasp the tenets of faith. Through the Moody courses, teachers gained insight into the importance of biblical content for transformation rather than just for its value as biblical literacy. Even teachers who were degreed in education were challenged to new levels as teachers learned to be reflective about their learning and teaching. The benefit Dr. Johnson's work far exceeded expectations.

Prior to the program, teachers had worked closely within their departments and knew one another well. They had experienced training programs together, but those had been largely skill driven. Because teachers enrolled as cohorts, Dr. Johnson's classes created a community of Christian educators who appreciated the work and challenges of their colleagues in different age level and instructional departments. The change in the caliber of instruction at the church was obvious immediately. For those who fully enrolled in the Moody class as continuing education students, the completion of the one hundred hours of instruction meant that each class member received a certificate in Christian education from that institution, an accomplishment that was celebrated with the entire congregation.

The result of CORE was seen in the lives of the teachers and their students. By the end of the experience, every teacher had moved into leadership in some way (Enrichment). They helped other teachers, designed and executed projects, extended their abilities into other ministries, and were engaged in denominational work at all levels. Several individuals enrolled in a Bible college and seminary where they continued to expand their learning.

The four areas of CORE are the result of the Apostolic Church of God's re-visioning its Christian education program. CORE was born as the leadership of Apostolic Church of God codified the experience and expanded it to include additional options at the Refining and Enrichment levels. The quantitative and qualitative research that went into the finalization of CORE led to the design of this sustainable Christian education training model. Every phase of CORE has been shown to enhance the passion born of transformative teaching.

A Revised Vision and Process

The challenge for church leaders and congregations is to reposition the teaching ministry so that local churches are better able to inspire and prepare congregants to live as faithful people who are called by a faithful God. Congregations can do this if, like the early church, they take seriously the call for the ministry of teaching. When the teaching ministry is central to the mission and work of each congregation, every encounter reveals some facet of who God is. The outcomes of worship, fellowship, and service will always honor God and spur members and visitors to seek God's will in every phase of their lives.

The CORE training model is comprehensive but manageable in all congregations. Its aim is to prepare teachers for the teaching ministry while recognizing the importance of their personal spiritual journeys. The four modules—Call, Orientation, Refining, and Enrichment— will vary based on the time schedule of the church and the creativity of church leaders. Call can be incorporated into the church's existing program for new members. It can also be developed for a whole-church focus that leads members into all areas of Christian service. Orientation is specifically for those who desire to teach, but it can be developed in segments so that it is not overwhelming to new teachers. Refining and Enrichment can be offered in flexible formats. Regardless of how the Christian education department decides to engage in CORE, the program will be beneficial.

The Call and Orientation phases of CORE establish the foundation for enhancing teacher understandings of faith, Bible knowledge, and teaching skills. While each phase of CORE is specific, the program has great flexibility. Increasingly, from Refining to Enrichment, teachers are given more opportunities to direct their own learning. To take full advantage of the CORE program of sustainable teacher preparation, ministry leaders must listen with discerning ears for evidence of teacher growth as well as new ideas that will enhance the Christian education department. When suggestions by teachers are appropriate, leaders should facilitate incorporating these ideas into existing or new programs. Leaders must be careful not to discourage teachers who have been empowered to learn new concepts and try new strategies. They are eager to share what they are learning and space should be provided for them to do that.

The Power of Repositioning God's Word

This foundational knowledge of God through the Bible must undergird the teaching ministry. God's desire is that we "love the LORD thy God with all thine heart, and with all thy soul, and with all thy might" (Deuteronomy 6:5). When teachers realize that they are not just relaying information, but presenting the Divine and Holy God who invites each learner to love Him totally, their teaching will reflect that truth. Helping learners know God is not an option; it is a requirement. It requires that the Word of God not just be on teachers' hearts; it must inundate the fiber of their being.

Knowing God's Word through personal encounter is a command and is the only real way to embrace the call to the teaching ministry. The eternal truths of the Bible transform the teacher and, in turn, transform the teaching encounter so that teachers can design and present lessons that enable the Word to be hidden in learners' hearts. Those involved in the teaching ministry must do more than just read the passage for a given lesson. They must be students of the Bible who seek its wisdom and guidance daily for themselves. Bible-centered teaching transforms the teacher to bring more to the learning environment than just an acquaintance with the content.

When churches adopt the CORE training program, they are creating a Christian education infrastructure and should expect the results to be fruitful for the entire ministry. Leadership gained through the Enrichment process provides real help to the ministry. By building capacity to support the teaching ministry, teachers are led through a process that increases their faith, utilizes their gifts, and enhances the faith community exponentially.

Summary

Throughout the Bible, we see the power of teaching to transform lives. Paul's epistles taught new converts about their relationship to God and each other. Preaching, as on the day of Pentecost, still causes people to ask, "What must I do to be saved?" (Acts 2:38). But the church is tasked with not only calling people to salvation but leading them to live in ways that denote increased faith in Jesus Christ. This latter task is accomplished through the collective ministries of the church, which are established by God to edify His body. It was teaching that emboldened the early church as they faced bloody massacres and expulsions from family and country. Through the power of teaching, Stephen, Philip, and others were able to accept ministry responsibilities not only to feed the widows (Acts 6) but to feed the Word to the lost (Acts 7 and 8).

Elevate the CORE has advocated for the CORE approach to Christian education in the local church because through it churches can develop effective Christian Education ministries where leaders focus on the transformative purposes of congregational teaching. Through CORE, teachers will effectively help students grow in their faith. With CORE, Christian educators are able to deliver the message of Christ in ways that draw others to service and worship. As a result of CORE, the Christian education ministry will undergo a radical change that will nurture growth and realize an increasing consistency in the faith of the congregation.

Consider:

1. What do you see as lacking in the training for Christian education programs you have experienced?
2. What resources and assistance do you envision needing in order to make CORE a reality for your congregation?
3. Who would you place on a leadership team to develop the CORE model at your church? Who would you consult?

APPENDIX A

Survey Questions

These following youth and adult survey questions were developed by Dr. Dale Johnson of Moody Bible Institute and are modified here. They are offered as suggestions of the information teachers may wish to know about participants. Questions should be adapted to accommodate specific groups and situations. A word of caution: While the original intent of these surveys was to gather information early in the class encounter, many people today are concerned with how much and how often personal information is requested as well as the format such questions take. Consider whether your group might respond better to being asked some of these questions as part of class introductions rather than requesting an online or print submission of all questions at once especially if multiple teachers are requesting the information.

YOUTH MINISTRY SURVEY QUESTIONS

Contact Information
Name
Address
Email
Social Media
Phone

Personal and Family Information
Age
School grade
School name

Father's name?
Mother's name?
Guardian's name?
Siblings?

Do any members of your family attend church with you?

Spiritual Relationship and Biblical Knowledge

1. My Relationship with Jesus Christ (check one):
   a. I have committed my life to Jesus Christ as Savior and Lord, and desire to obey Him in every area of my life.
   b. I have a basic understanding of who Jesus Christ is, but I am not yet ready to commit my life to Him.
   c. I know very little about Jesus Christ, but I am interested in learning more about Him.
2. My Knowledge and Understanding of the Bible (check one):
   a. Fairly strong - Desire to dig deep.
   b. A handle on the basics - Desire to know more
   c. Really new to me- Desire to get on board

3. My Church Involvement (activities, groups, auxiliaries, etc.)
4. My School Involvement (include groups and activities in addition to classes)

Interests and Involvement

1. Other Involvement (employment, clubs, leisure activities, etc.):
2. My favorite hobby/spare time activity is:
3. My favorite type of music is:
4. My favorite music group/artist is:
5. My favorite movie is:
6. My favorite TV show is:
7. My favorite magazine is:

Other

1. Two people I most respect and look up to are:
2. If I could ask God one question, it would be:
3. Some things that really concern me are:
4. My closest friend(s) in this church/group is/are:

ADULT MINISTRY SURVEY QUESTIONS

Personal and Family Information
Name
Address
Email
Social Media
Phone

General Age Group:

❑ 20 -29
❑ 30 -39
❑ 40 - 49
❑ 50 – 59
❑ 60 – 69
❑ 70 +

Status:

❑ Single (Never married)
❑ Single (Divored)
❑ Single (Widowed)
❑ Married
❑ Spouse's name – Does your spouse attend this church?

Children
How many
Ages/school levels (Preschool, elementary, middle school, high school, adults)
Employment (full-time, part-time, homemaker, student, unemployed,

self-employed, other)
Church Involvement (auxiliaries, groups, activities)

Spiritual Relationship and Biblical Knowledge

1. My Relationship With Jesus Christ (check one):
    a.   I have committed my life to Jesus Christ as Savior and Lord, and desire to obey Him in every area of my life.
    b.   I have a basic understanding of who Jesus Christ is, but I am not yet ready to commit my life to Him.
    c.   I know very little about Jesus Christ, but I am interested in learning more about Him.

2. My Knowledge and Understanding of the Bible (check one):
    a.   Fairly strong - Desire to dig deep.
    b.   A handle on the basics - Desire to know more
    c.   Really new to me- Desire to get on board

3. My closest friend(s) in this church/group is/are:

Interests and Involvement
1. Other Interests (clubs, sports, hobbies, leisure activities, etc.):
2. Favorite hobby/spare time activity is:
3. Favorite type of music is:
4. Favorite music group/artist is:
5. Favorite movie is:
6. Favorite TV show is:
7. Favorite magazine is:

Other
1. Two people I most respect and look up to are:
2. If I could ask God one question, it would be:
3. Some things that really concern me are:

The RISE Model

This lesson plan is based on Genesis 29 and 30 as well as the book, *Let Her Life Speak* by Dr. Rosa Sailes (available at Keys to the Kingdom Publishing, LLC, https://ktkpublishing.com or Amazon.com).

LESSONS FROM LEAH

Objectives: At the end of this session, participants will be able to:
- Explore Bible study methods that they can use in personal study
- Discuss their views of Leah
- Identify the family traditions and social codes at work in Leah's life
- Embrace attributes of God identified in Leah's children's names

R – Ready: Use either of the options below to prepare participants for learning. The object is to help participants identify their prior knowledge and trigger their prior experiences with either the Bible passage or the topic for discussion. Use either option 1 or 2, or both.

Option 1:
- Ask how many participants watch *The Bachelor, The Bachelorette,* or *The Proposal.*
- Ask who would, or would not, be a contestant on such a program and why? How do these programs reflect or shape society's opinion of marriage today?

Option 2:
- Have the class brainstorm a list of modern wedding traditions.

- After creating the list, ask which of these have changed from generation to generation and how? (Example: Wedding gowns have changed so that brides may or may not wear a veil.)

I – Ignite: Introduce the biblical text or specific topic and the outcomes that are anticipated.

- Explain that a study of Genesis 29-30 focuses on the marriage customs of the time and explores the marriage of Leah to Jacob.
- Ask participants to share their opinions of Leah using the following questions:
  - Before this reading, what was your opinion and image of Leah (physically, mentally, emotionally, etc.)
  - What do you think shaped your opinion of Leah?
  - Based on their pre-class reading, what questions or curiosities did they find about marriage in biblical times. Make a list of the issues raised but do not answer them.

S – Search: Explore the biblical text, lesson, or topic using brain-based strategies and intentional spiritual engagement.

Exercise 1
- Divide the class into groups. Give each group a brief article on one of these topics:

  - o Bet ab
  - o Wedding and betrothal customs
  - o Wives – primary and secondary
  - o Childbearing
  - o The importance of sons

- Have each group read their article and then allow participants to use the 5+1 technique (Who, What, When, Why, Where and How) to record their findings. Allow groups to report briefly.
- Clarify any misunderstandings about the traditions or customs, how they are used in Genesis 29-30, and how such traditions would be viewed today.

Exercise 2

- Lead participants through a review of Leah's children's names, their meanings, and her thinking/situation when she decided on each name.
- Allow the class to explain how each name relates to an attribute of God.
- Pass out a list of modern day scenarios. Examples might include a couple who is facing divorce or a person who is being bullied or harassed on the job.
- Have participants work in groups, to examine their scenario and determine, based on Leah's children's names, which attribute of God is helpful in that scenario.
- Ask participants to complete a personal chart using one or more of the names to explain what each name means or can mean for their lives. Allow those who wish to share to do so.
- Pose the question of whether Leah's life was centered in triumph or tragedy and why.
- As the class session wraps up, ask how learning more about God through our experiences can help us in developing positive rather than negative attitudes even in our worst situations.
- Finally answer any questions that participants might have.

E – Extend: Provide activities that help participants continue to think about and act on their learning beyond the classroom.

- End class by encouraging participants to do one or more of the following prior to the next class session:
  - Using the name you selected on your chart, identify one or more Scriptures that give insight into that attribute of God. Incorporate that Scripture into your daily devotion in the coming week.
  - Leah's experiences led her to know God more fully. Take time this week to journal about how you are learning about God more each day?
  - Leah cried out to God through the names of her children? Journal or create a list this week of ways you are crying out to God.

Endnotes

SECTION 1

1 Neil McQueen, "Is Sunday School Going Extinct?" https://www.sundayresources.net/neil/2009/06/25/is-sunday-school-going-extinct-or/, (Accessed 7/6/2018); David Kinnaman, "Sunday School Is Changing in Under-the-Radar But Significant Ways," https://www.barna.org/barna-update/article/5-barna-update/175-sunday-school-is-changing-in-under-the-radar-but-significant-ways#.Uq4CRHmA2Uk. (Accessed 12/15/2013.)

2 My work with churches and the church community included five years as the Director of Editorial Curriculum at Urban Ministries, Inc. I am grateful for that experience as well as the opportunity to work as part of the writing team with the National Council of Churches Uniform Lesson Series. For four years, I worked collaboratively with outstanding educators, theologians and pastors who represented independent and denominational publishing houses from across the United States. My time as a freelance writer, as well as my denominational work in publications, have allowed me to more fully appreciate the rigor and research required for the creation of curricular materials by independent and denominational publishing houses.

3 Gary Shogren, Why Didn't I Drop Out of Church, http://christmycovenant.com/why-didnt-i-drop-out-of-church/. (Accessed 6/7/2018); Focus on the Family Findings, Religious Affiliation and Retention, Executive Summary, August 2013, p. 1, http://www.focusonthefamily.com/about_us/focus-findings/religion-and-culture/~/media/images/about-us/focus-findings/FF%20-%20Millenial%20Faith%20Retention%20FINAL.ashx. (Accessed 12/15/2013.)

4 Focus on the Family, 5; Barna Group, "Five Reasons Millennials Stay Connected to Church," https://www.barna.org/barna-update/millennials/635-5-reasons-millennials-stay-connected-to-church#.Uq398HmA2Uk. (Accessed 2/15/13).

5 Ibid.

6 Margaret Poloma, "A Quick Question: Is Pentecostalism Christianity's Next Reformation?" in Hartford Institute for Religion and Research, http://hirr.hartsem.edu/research/quick_question32.html. (Accessed 6/7/2018.)

7 Charles Foster, *Educating Congregations: The Future of Christian Education*, (Nashville: Abingdon Press, 1994) p. 21; Focus on the Family, p. 2.

8 The AFCARS Report, (Washington, DC: U.S. Department of Health and Human Services, 2011), https://www.acf.hhs.gov/sites/default/files/cb/afcarsreport19.pdf, (Accessed 6/10/2018.) Emancipation means that youth who were minors were allowed to live on their own despite their age or they became too old for the foster care system.

9 Child Welfare Information Gateway, Foster Care Statistics 2016, (Washington, DC: U.S. Department of Health and Human Services Children's Bureau, 2018), https://www.childwelfare.gov/pubs/factsheets/foster/. (Accessed 5/16/2018.)

10 Victor Ochieng, "Why 59% of Millennials Are Leaving the Church," http://

yourblackworld.net/2017/02/20/why-59-of-millennials-are-leaving-church/. (Accessed 5/16/2018.)

11   Focus on the Family, pp. 2, 4; Pew Research, U.S. Religious Landscape Study: Religious Affiliation, Chapter 1, http://www.pewforum.org/2008/02/01/chapter-1-the-religious-composition-of-the-united-states/#the-decline-of-american-protestantism. (Accessed 6/7/2018.)

12   Gregory Smith and Jessica Pumphrey, "When Americans Say They Believe in God, What Do They Mean?" in Pew Research Study, April 25, 2018. http://www.pewforum.org/2018/04/25/when-americans-say-they-believe-in-god-what-do-they-mean/. (Accessed 6/3/2018.)

13   2010 Report of Religious Bodies (Footnote), http://www.thearda.com/rcms2010/r/c/08/rcms2010_08113_county_name_2010.asp. (Accessed 6/7/2018.) The African American church seems to follow the basic patterns found in other churches even though African Americans, and particularly Black Pentecostals, are often not included in the research studies.

14   Focus on the Family, p. 3.

15   Scott L. Thumma, Megachurches Today 2000: Summary of Data from the Faith Community Today 2000 Project, http://hirr.hartsem.edu/megachurch/faith_megachurches_FACTsummary.html. (Accessed 12/30/2013.)

16   Elena Larsen, CyberFaith: How Americans Pursue Religion Online, http://www.pewinternet.org/2001/12/23/cyberfaith-how-americans-pursue-religion-online/. (Accessed 6/7/2018.)

17   The United Methodist Reporter, Recently Read: COB and Wall Street Journal Take on Online Communion, November 16, 2013, http://unitedmethodistreporter.com/2013/11/16/recently-read-cob-wall-street-journal-take-online-communion/. (Accessed 6/7/2018.)

18   Michael S. Beates, Church Shopping: A Discussion of the Problems Around Churches Today, http://www.gsclc.org/hbshopping.asp. (Accessed 12/30/2013.)

19   Scott L. Thumma, "Megachurch Report"; Hartford Institute for Religion Research, "Megachurch Report Shows Continued Growth But Many Challenges," https://www.hartsem.edu/2015/12/megachurch-report-shows-continued-growth-but-many-challenges/. (Accessed 6/7/2018.)

20   Jeffrey M. Jones, "Sept. 11 Effects, Though Largely Faded, Persist," in Gallup Poll Report, http://www.gallup.com/poll/9208/Sept-Effects-Though-Largely-Faded-Persist.aspx. (Accessed 12/16/2013.)

21   Ibid.

22   Foster, 34. Post-Christian means that the rules of operating society are no longer established by the Church and church life. Sundays are no longer sacred; they are commercially viable. It is erroneous to believe that post-Christian means that Christianity and the Bible have lost their relevance. While our communities may be inundated with religious and life-style choices that are counter-cultural to the Bible, the power of the Bible and the Gospel message has not been diminished. The purpose of teaching ministry is to proclaim that power more effectively in faith communities and to the world.

23   Chris Hubbub, "Churches Seek Relevance As Americans Turn Aside From

Organized Religion" in LaCrosse Tribune.com, http://lacrossetribune.com/news/local/churches-seek-relevance-as-many-americans-turn-away-from-organized/article_d7b1a3a8-99b6-11e2-9f6b-001a4bcf887a.html. (Accessed 2/15/2013.)

24   Debra Dean Murphy, *Teaching That Transforms: Worship as the Heart of Christian Education*, (Grand Rapids, Michigan: Brazos Press, 2004), p. 18.

25   Editors of the Encyclopedia Britannica, "Robert Raikes: British Philanthropist," https://www.britannica.com/biography/Robert-Raikes. (Accessed 6/7/2018.)

26   Timothy Larson, "Christian History: When Did Sunday Schools Start?" in Christianity Today,http://www.christianitytoday.com/ch/asktheexpert/when-didsundayschoolstart.html. (Accessed 12/17/2013.)

27   David Kinnaman, Sunday School is Changing in Under-the-Radar But Significant Ways, https://www.barna.org/barna-update/article/5-barna-update/175-sunday-school-is-changing-in-under-the-radar-but-significant-ways#.Uq4CRH-mA2Uk. (Accessed 12/15/2013).

28   Lifeway, "About Lifeway Vacation Bible School," http://www.lifeway.com/Article/about-lifeway-vacation-bible-school. (Accessed 12/30/2013.)

29   Stephen Gertz, "From Beer to Bibles to VBS: How America Got Its Favorite Summer Tradition," posted 6/1/2003, https://g.christianbook.com/ns/pdf/201706/HistoryofVBS2.pdf?event=VBS|1000259. (Accessed 6/7/2018.)

30   Ibid.

31   Ibid.

32   Ibid.

33   David Kinnaman, Sunday School is Changing in Under-the-Radar But Significant Ways, https://www.barna.org/barna-update/article/5-barna-update/175-sunday-school-is-changing-in-under-the-radar-but-significant-ways#.Uq4CRH-mA2Uk. (Accessed 12/15/2013).

34   I served as a consultant on the Uniform Lesson Series for five years while in the employ of Urban Ministries.

35   David C. Cook has purchased several companies and is now has other companies under its control and has become the largest publisher of Sunday School Curriculum.

36   Urban Ministries, Inc., "Who We Are," https://urbanministries.com/our-story/ (Accessed 6/7/2018)

37   David Kinnaman, Sunday School is Changing in Under-the-Radar But Significant Ways, https://www.barna.org/barna-update/article/5-barna-update/175-sunday-school-is-changing-in-under-the-radar-but-significant-ways#.Uq4CRH-mA2Uk. (Accessed 12/15/2013).

38   While the format, purpose and scope of denominational Sunday School materials are similar, denominational curricula do not always use the NCC frameworks.

39   Murphy, p. 10.

40   Murphy, p. 11.

41   William Seymour College, "Heritage, Faith, Legacy," (Laurel Maryland: William Seymour College Board of Trustees Information Package, 2013); Camille Ryan and Julie Siebens, "Educational Attainment in the United States: 2009," Issued

February 2012, http://www.census.gov/prod/2012pubs/p20-566.pdf. (Accessed 12/17/2013.) Only 7% of people raised in Pentecostal homes will likely complete a 4-year college degree. The 2009 American Community Survey 2009 indicated that 28% of the general population reported having a bachelor's degree or higher

42   Seymour.

43   Center for Disease Control and Prevention, Assuring Healthy Caregivers: A Public Health Approach to Translating Research into Practice: The Re-Aim Framework, https://www.cdc.gov/aging/pdf/caregiving_monograph.pdf. (Accessed 10/2/2017.)

44   Amanda Noss, Household Income 2012: American Community Survey Briefs, pp. 1, 4, https://www.census.gov/library/publications/2013/acs/acsbr12-02.html. (Accessed 5/24/2017); Bureau of Labor Statistics, "American Time Use Survey," http://www.bls.gov/tus/charts/. (Accessed 5/16/2018.)

45   Bureau of Labor Statistics, "Time Use Survey."

46   Bureau of Labor Statistics, "The Employment Situation – May 2018," https://www.bls.gov/news.release/pdf/empsit.pdf. (Accessed 5/16/2018.)

47   Foster, 34.

48   Maria Harris, *Fashion Me A People: Curriculum in the Church*, (Louisville: Westminster/John Knox Press, 1989), p. 33.

49   Given the duality so prevalent in the church, this book attempts to use the words "volunteers," "lay persons," and "unordained persons" interchangeably only when the terms "member," "teacher," or "Christian educator" fail to be sufficiently descriptive. This is not to categorize people or to isolate vocation, but to identify workers.

50   Michelle Van Loon, "Volunteers – An Oxymoron" in Christianity Today, July 13, 2010, http://www.christianitytoday.com/women/2010/july/church-volunteers-oxymoron.html. (Accessed 12/17/2013.)

51   David L. Bartlett, *Paul's Vision for the Teaching Church*, (Valley Forge: Judson Press, 1977), p. 37.

52   Foster, p. 25.

53   Harris, p. 17.

54   Harris, p. 17.

55   Bartlett, p. 13.

56   Murphy, p. 12-13.

SECTION 2

57   Richard Robert Osmer, T*eaching for Faith: A Guide for Teachers of Adult Classes*, (Louisville, Kentucky: Westminster/John Knox Press, 1992) p. 15.

58   A. W. Tozer, *The Knowledge of the Holy*, (New York: Harper Collins Publishing, 1961), p. vii.

59   Howard W. Stone and James O. Duke, *How to Think Theologically*, (Minneapolis: Fortress Press, 1996) p. 51. This is an adaptation of Stone and Duke's framework where faith is substituted for reason. This is not because reason is not

necessary but because the clarity (reason) needed to examine life is anchored in faith.

60   Stone and Duke, p. 119.

61   William Shakespeare, *Hamlet*, Act 1, Scene 3, http://shakespeare.mit.edu/hamlet/full.html. (Accessed 5/24/2017).

62   Israel Galindo, *The Craft of Teaching*, (Minneapolis: Fortress Pres, 1996), p. 15.

63   Dottie Rambo, "He Looked Beyond My Faults and Saw My Needs," https://www.lyriczz.com/lyrics/dottie-rambo/61211-he-looked-beyond-my-faults/. (Accessed 5/10/2016.)

64   Stone and Duke, p. 2.

65   U. S. Department of Education Office of Technology Education, National Education Technology Plan, Executive Summary, p. 1, http://www.ed.gov/technology/netp-2010/executive-summary. (Accessed 2/7/2014.)

66   Scott L. Thumma, "Virtually Religious: Technology and Internet Use in American Congregations" in Hartford Institute for Religion Research, http://hirr.hartsem.edu/megachurch/faith_megachurches_FACTsummary.html. (Accessed 12/30/2013.)

67   Marc Prensky, "Digital Natives, Digital Immigrants" in On the Horizon (MCB University Press, Vol. 9 No. 5, October 2001), p. 1. http://marcprensky.com/writing/Prensky%20-%20Digital%20Natives,%20Digital%20Immigrants%20-%20Part1.pdf. (Accessed 5/8/2017.)

68   James A. Beane, *Affect in the Curriculum: Toward Democracy, Dignity, and Diversity*, (New York: Teachers College Columbia University, 1990), p. 8.

69   Adele Berlin and Marc Zvi Brettler, "Psalms" in *Jewish Study Bible*, (Oxford: University Press, 2004), p 1284 note.

70   Thomas Long, "Exegesis" in *The Interpreters' Handbook*, (Nashville: Abingdon Press, 2008), p. 19.

71   "Transformation" in *Oxford English Dictionary*, http://www.oed.com.covers.chipublib.org/view/Entry/204743?redirectedFrom=transformation&. (Accessed 2/8/2014.)

72   A. W. Tozer, *The Knowledge of the Holy*, p. 69.

73   A. W. Tozer, *The Knowledge of the Holy*, pp. 70-71.

74   Paul Enns, "Bibliology: Doctrine of the Bible" in *Moody Handbook of Theology*, (Chicago: Moody Press, 2008), p. 157.

75   A. W. Tozer, *The Knowledge of the Holy*, pp. 26-27.

76   Stone and Duke, p. 2.

77   James P. Boise, "Abstract of Systematic Theology" in *Christian Classics Ethereal Library*, http://www.ccel.org/ccel/boyce/theology.html. (Accessed 7/28/14.)

78   Stone and Duke, p. 70.

79   Long, p. 18.

80   A. W. Tozer, *The Pursuit of God*, (Camp Hill, Pennsylvania: Wing Spread Publishers, 1993), p. 70.

81   Wayne Grudem, *Systematic Theology: An Introduction to Biblical Doc-

trines, (Grand Rapids, Michigan: Zondervan, 1994) p. 27.

82   Grudem, p. 26.

83   "Biblical Criticism," Encyclopedia Britannica, www.britannica.com/topic/biblical-criticism. (Accessed 6/4/2018.)

84   Ronald J. Allen, "Form Criticism" in Paul Scott Wilson, ed., *The New Interpreters' Handbook of Preaching*, (Nashville: Abingdon Press, 2008), pp. 24-25.

85   John H. Hayes and Carl R. Holladay, *Biblical Exegesis: Beginner's Handbook*, (Atlanta: John Knox Press, 1987), p. 45.

86   Allen, Ronald J., p. 25.

87   Mark Allen Powell, *What Is Narrative Criticism?* (Minneapolis: Fortress Press, 1990), p. 19.

88   My introduction to this method occurred over 50 years ago when a history professor at Northern Illinois University suggested that it would be helpful in passing his class. I have long since forgotten his name, but I have always appreciated, used, and shared the acronym because of its investigative power. (I also passed the class.) I now know that modern methodologies relate this process to human or cultural geography.

89   Osmer, p. 11.

90   Robert B. Costello, Editor-in-chief, "Praxis," in Random House *Webster's College Dictionary*, (New York: Random House, 1992), p. 1060.

91   Parenthetical statement.

92   James Weldon Johnson, "Listen Lord" from *God's Trombones*, http://poetry-archive.com/j/the_creation.html. (Accessed July 27, 2014.)

93   U. S. Department of Education, "Prepare My Child for School: Typical Language Accomplishments for Children, Birth to Age 6 – Helping Your Child Become a Reader." http://www2.ed.gov/parents/academic/help/reader/part9.html. (Accessed 10/27/2012); Tania K. Cowling, "Physical Development in Children Age 0-3," http://www.ehow.com/how-does_5269762_physical-development-children-age.html. (Accessed 10/30/, 2012).

94   Don Tapscott, "How Digital Technology Has Changed the Brain," November 10, 2008, http://www.businessweek.com/stories/2008-11-10/how-digital-technology-has-changed-the-brainbusinessweek-business-news-stock-market-and-financial-advice. (Accessed 6/25/2014).

95   In 1999 the Sensational Nightingales recorded a song by this title. Johnny Cash is also reported to have recorded this song. It is not clear whether the phrase in common church use pre-dated these recordings.

96   Tozer, *Knowledge of the Holy*, p. vii.

SECTION 3

97   Spiros Zodhiates, Executive ed., "Kaleo" in *Hebrew-Greek Key Study Bible*, (Chattanooga, Tennessee: AMG Publishers, 2008), p. 2161.

98   David J. Greenhaw, "Call" in Wilson, Paul Scott, ed., *New Interpreters Handbook of Preaching*, (Nashville, Tennessee: Abingdon Press, 2008) p. 224.

99   Ibid.

100   Bible Gateway, https://www.biblegateway.com/. (Accessed 7/19/2014.)

101   Eric Jensen, *Teaching with the Brain in Mind*, (Alexandria, Virginia: Association of Supervision and Curriculum Development, 1998), pp. 92 (diagram), 100,

102   Eric Jensen, "Inside the Teenage Brain" in How Much Do We Really Know About the Brain? http://www.pbs.org/wgbh/pages/frontline/shows/teenbrain/work/how.html. (Accessed 5/10/2018); Jensen, Teaching with the Brain in Mind, pp. 8, 115-118.

103   Howard Gardner, *Frames of Mind: The Theory of Multiple Intelligences*, (New York: Basic Books, 2011), pp. 8-9.

104   Gardner, p. xviii.

105   Gardner, p. 64.

106   James Bellanca and Robin Fogarty, *Blueprints for Thinking in the Cooperative Classroom* (2nd ed.), (Palatine, Illinois: Skylight Publishing, Inc., 1991), p. 40.

107   Jensen, *Teaching with the Brain in Mind*, p. 43.

108   Jensen, *Teaching with the Brain in Mind*, p. 46.

109   Jensen, *Teaching with the Brain in Mind*, p. 42.

110   John C. Maxwell in Brainyquotes, http://www.brainyquote.com/quotes/quotes/j/johncmaxw383606.html. (Accessed 8/31/2014).

111   Osmer, 12.

112   I was the director and the program was developed under my leadership.